# THE STRENGTHS OF AFRICAN AMERICAN FAMILIES

## *Twenty-Five Years Later*

## Robert B. Hill

Foreword by

Andrew Billingsley

University Press of America,® Inc.
Lanham • New York • Oxford

**Copyright © 1999**
**University Press of America,® Inc.**
4720 Boston Way
Lanham, Maryland 20706

12 Hid's Copse Rd.
Cumnor Hill, Oxford OX2 9JJ

**Library of Congress Cataloging-in-Publication Data**

Hill, Robert Bernard.
The strengths of African American families : twenty-five years later /
Robert B. Hill ; foreword by Andrew Billingsley.
p.    cm.
Rev. ed. of: The strengths of Black families. lst ed. 1972.
Includes bibliographical references.
l.  Afro-American families.  I.  Hill, Robert Bernard, Strengths of
Black families.  II. Title.
(E185.86.H66  1998)   306.85'089'96073—dc21   98-30600 CIP

ISBN 0-7618-1250-4 (cloth: alk. ppr.)
ISBN 0-7618-1251-2 (pbk: alk. ppr.)

♾™ The paper used in this publication meets the minimum
requirements of American National Standard for Information
Sciences—Permanence of Paper for Printed Library Materials,
ANSI Z39.48—1984

*To the Unsung Heroes
in the African American Village*

# CONTENTS

# FOREWORD

I was honored when Robert Hill asked me to write the foreword to his pathbreaking volume, "The Strengths of Black Families." The success of that slim volume has been remarkable. Then it was so uncommon as to seem heretical to utter the expression "strengths " in connection with analyses of African American families. Today, twenty-five years later, not only is there a common framework for analysis of African American families, but students of other cultural traditions have increasingly been encouraged to look for "strengths" among families, even those who are being studied because they present problems of one sort or another to themselves, their communities, or the larger society. In this regard Bob Hill's work has been truly pace-setting, and although he might not be given the recognition for this contribution, those who follow these matters closely must take their hats off to him. Moreover, among students of African American families, both black and white, Hill's work has been indispensable for teaching, for seminars, and for our own analyses.

Now comes this new twenty-fifth year update; it is phenomenal. Many have long awaited this update, because we have known that Bob was working on it. It is characteristic of him to take his time, do thorough analyses, take into consideration critiques of his work, and, most especially, take into consideration changing conditions and circumstances before bringing out this new edition. It was well worth the wait. Three facets of this new work bring it forcefully to the attention of scholars, professionals, policy analysts, community leaders, and lay leaders alike. First, this new book is bigger. While Hill described the five basic strengths of black families in the earlier edition: strong kinship bonds, strong work orientation, adaptability of family roles, high achievement orientation, and strong religious orientation, he devoted only a few paragraphs of exposition to each. Indeed the entire first volume was less than a hundred pages. This new volume expands considerably on his documentation and explanation of each of these characteristic strengths. Each one is given the full length chapter it deserves. More important still, in this work, he has given greater depth to the context of these family values in several other well-chosen and well-written chapters. He takes care to lay out for the reader his overall "Solutions Framework." In this brilliant exposition, Hill takes the reader into the thought processes he brings to his work. In it he lays out the basis for the reader to understand, to critique, and to differ with his own conclusions and conceptualizations. It is a framework that guides the entire book. We are treated to Hill's view that the historical perspective, the ecological perspective, cultural perspective, problem identification and solutions identification are all necessary elements of a full understanding of African American family life. He explains each of these concepts fully, and, for the first time, he extends his historical perspective to embrace the new scholarship on the African heritage of African American families. Before reintroducing us to the five historic strengths, he gives us a chapter on social class, clearing up much of the confusion in the use and misuse of this valuable concept.

A second impressive feature of this book, next to the fullness of its exposition, is the thoroughness with which it is documented. We are not left to rely on Hill's own studies, analyses, and perspectives, but he draws generously on pioneering studies that other scholars have done during the past twenty-five years. Such studies improve our understanding of African American families and further enlighten his own treatment.

The third distinctive feature of this work is that in addition to being well-documented, it is well-written. That is no mean feat in the social sciences literature. Never does he allow the data, or the social science to becloud the clarity of his exposition, and although we have lauded the book for being larger than the original, it should be emphasized that Bob Hill is exceptionally economic in his discussion--just long enough to clarify the concept, and no longer.

Foreword

It is for these reasons, that *The Strengths of African American Families: Twenty-Five Years Later,* will make such a profound contribution to the literature and, more importantly, to the understanding and enlightenment of readers across a wide spectrum. Teachers, social workers, counselors, community activists, policy makers, and the general reader will find this a most useful, authoritative, and readable exposition of the African American family situation. Personally, I can hardly wait to use it in my classes, lectures, seminars, and conversations with friends and strangers alike.

ANDREW BILLINGSLEY

# PREFACE

My earlier volume *The Strengths of Black Families* was published in 1972, a time of depressing disparities between blacks and whites. Joblessness among blacks was twice as high as whites. Rates of poverty and single-parent families were three times higher among blacks than whites. The conclusions of the 1965 Moynihan Report, that the family structure of blacks was crumbling because of a surge in one-parent families, were still being widely discussed. It was not, therefore, surprising that my work would be criticized by some commentators as "romanticizing" black families, since "everyone" knew that black families had no assets or strengths worth writing about.

Twenty-five years later, although the gaps in unemployment, poverty, and one-parent families between blacks and whites persist, the severity of these problems in the black community appears to have worsened. Moreover, new social problems have emerged: the availability of guns to youth, teen violence, open-air drug trafficking, a crack epidemic, AIDS, and homelessness. While jobs are exported from inner-cities, drugs and weapons are imported. Innocent children and adults are wounded or killed as a result of drive-by shootings, and many residents feel that their communities are in a state of siege. If it was difficult to understand how a social scientist could write about any "strengths" among black families in 1972, a sequel to that work in 1997 might be expected to be met with wider disbelief.

Yet, the reasons I wrote my 1972 work continue to hold a generation later. First, I still believe that the conventional depiction of black families in the media and in the social science literature is unbalanced. The typical portrayal focuses on the weaknesses or deficiencies of a disadvantaged minority of black families--with little or no consideration of the majority. For example, there is a fixation on the nonworking poor (or "underclass"), that excludes examination of the larger working class (that is, the working poor and near-poor) who often live in the same communities, or, excessive attention is paid to the two out of ten black families on welfare, or on the one out of ten black adolescent females who had babies out of wedlock. Second, I was concerned that most stories on the black community in the media or research studies were interested in explaining why blacks fail and underachieve, and not why the majority of low-income blacks are able to achieve against the odds. These analyses rarely seek answers to such questions as: why eight out of ten black families are not on welfare; why nine out of ten black adolescents do not have children out of wedlock, and why two out of three black males do not have contact with the criminal justice system. If one were truly interested in replicating successful inner-city achievement, I contend that greater attention would be given to identifying factors that make such resilience possible.

Third, I felt that typical analyses of black families are mainly interested in identifying problems, not solutions. They usually end after presenting statistics that document the severity or prevalence of a problem. Clearly, the first step in solving any problem is to acknowledge that it exists and to examine its severity. However, after the problems have been identified, the analysts rarely proceed to identify and discuss solutions or remedies to those problems. As a result, most readers are left with the feeling that the situation is hopeless, that little can be done to enhance black youth or their families. In short, the conventional analysis of black families leads to paralysis!

Fourth, because many low-income black families clearly need to be strengthened, I believe that one of the most effective ways to make them stronger is to identify policies and programs that reinforce existing strengths and resilient coping mechanisms. Thus, a focus on strengths is solution-oriented. It attempts to identify strategies--within the black community and in the larger society-- that make families stronger.

In short, the main purpose of *The Strengths of Black Families* and this sequel is to offer concerned parents, youth, community activists, service providers, and policy makers possible solutions to so-called intractable problems among black families. Both works identify resilient or protective factors in the black community and in the larger society that reduce the social problems of dropping out of school, teenage pregnancy, welfare dependence, drug addiction, violence, crime, and delinquency among black families.

Another objective of this sequel is to make the general public and research community aware of many unpublicized studies that have focused on the strengths and assets of families of color since the early 1970s. Such works have examined effective family functioning not only among middle-income but among low-income black families as well. Although they account for only a small fraction of all studies of black families, they have made important contributions to enhancing this nation's knowledge of the complex factors that affect the structure and functioning of African American families. Recent works by historians, anthropologists, sociologists, psychologists, social workers, urban planners, philosophers, and educators have provided many new insights into black family life. Unfortunately, these works are rarely cited or receive the "silent treatment" because their findings do not support popular stereotypes of African American families.

An important insight of these new works is that many of the effective coping strategies of contemporary black families are legacies from their African heritage. These studies have concluded that many positive attributes of today's black families, such as strong religious orientation, flexible family roles, extended- family networks, and informal adoption processes derive from African cultural patterns. I am especially grateful to Dr. Asa Hilliard, III, for alerting me to such African continuities after the publication in 1977 of my work *Informal Adoption Among Black Families.*

Recent works by historians have corrected a popular tendency to romanticize the past by assuming "a golden era" among blacks that never existed. Historical research has refuted the widespread belief that the high levels of black families headed by women and out-of-wedlock births are of recent origin by showing comparable data for blacks during the 1800s as well as the early 1900s. Moreover, historians have revealed that blacks were not passive victims of racial and economic oppression but were major agents of change in their quest for freedom and equality.

Most importantly, the past twenty-five years have yielded new insights into effective programs to aid black and low-income families. Unfortunately, this knowledge of effective family-strengthening strategies has not been incorporated into the national discourse about African American families. Thousands of community groups throughout the nation are demonstrating every day that it is possible to help low-income youth and their families to transform stumbling blocks into stepping-stones! Yet, most policy makers and practitioners do not know about these successful inner-city efforts.

Community-based organizations at national and local levels have devised effective strategies for strengthening African American families. The National Council of Negro Woman, under the dynamic leadership of Dr. Dorothy Height, has been in the forefront of this effort to celebrate the accomplishments of black families by holding Annual Black Family Reunions in Washington, D.C. and in various cities across the nation since 1986. A similar inspiring event was the historic Million Man March that was organized by Minister Louis Farrakhan on 16 October 1995 in Washington, D.C. It was publicized as a day of atonement for black men, a day to strengthen their commitment to their children, wives, friends, and families. The National Center for Neighborhood Enterprise (NCNE), founded by Robert L. Woodson, Sr., is another agency committed to empowering low-income groups--public housing residents, former gang members, and other grassroots leaders--by building on the strengths of the poor. NCNE established Achievement Against the Odds (AAO) awards to confer national recognition on the accomplishments of low-income individuals from all races.

More balanced portrayals of African American families occur regularly in various black-oriented publications, namely, *Ebony, Jet, Essence, Emerge, American Visions* magazines and the *Afro-American* and other black newspapers throughout the country.

Several TV and radio-talk shows also make important contributions to the discussion of solutions to black community problems. One of the most effective is the round-the-clock "Information is Power" program on the Radio One stations owned by Cathy Hughes in Washington, D.C. and Baltimore. Another positive public medium is the nationally-syndicated "Night Talk" radio program hosted by community activist Bob Law, who is also the founder of the "Respect Yourself" Youth Organization.

Unfortunately, such balance and sensitivity have not been achieved by mainstream broadcast and print media. They continue to devote disproportionate coverage to the negative features of black families or to extreme examples of dysfunctionality.

Clearly, many African American families have been severely destabilized over the past generation by high levels of unemployment, poverty, homelessness, teenage pregnancies, out-of-wedlock births, infant mortality, poor health, substance abuse, AIDS, crime, and violence. On the other hand, eight out of ten black families today are working class, middle class or upper class; two out of three women who head black families are in the labor force; and four out of five black families are not dependent on welfare. In short, the overwhelming majority of African American families are making positive contributions to society in spite of racism and other social and economic constraints.

This second edition of *The Strengths of Black Families* was written to answer several questions: (1) What important social and economic changes in black families have occurred over the past twenty-five years? (2) Which societal forces, policies, and programs have impeded or facilitated the functioning of African American families? (3) What cultural strengths and coping strategies in the African American community have helped low-income children, youth, and families to achieve against the odds? (4) What successful initiatives by community-based groups to strengthen black and low-income families are taking place across this nation? (5) Which policies of the larger society and self-help strategies in the African American community are needed to strengthen African American families during the twenty-first century?

The first chapter presents a comprehensive framework for understanding the contemporary situation of African American families and for developing solutions to many problems affecting the black community. Chapter two examines how the African cultural heritage has influenced the functioning of black families in America. The third chapter presents a critique of the misuse of the class concept in conventional analyses of black families. It then provides an overview of important class trends that have occurred among African American families during the past two decades. Chapters four through eight examine five strengths of black families and the respective contribution of each. The final chapter provides a brief conclusion and discusses implications for public policies and self-help strategies for strengthening African American families.

I would like to thank members of my immediate family for helping to make this book possible: my children, Bernard and Renee, for their constant encouragement and support; my wife, Barbara, for inspiring me over the years to complete this work; and, my mother, Marie, for continually exhibiting the strengths of a working-class parent in her children's daily lives.

**Robert B. Hill**

# Chapter 1

---

# SOLUTIONS FRAMEWORK

In order to understand the structure and functioning of contemporary African American families, we suggest that analysts incorporate a holistic or solutions framework. Our holistic framework comprises the following dimensions: (a) a historical perspective; (b) an ecological perspective; (c) a cultural perspective; (d) problems identification; and (e) solutions identification.

## HISTORICAL PERSPECTIVE

A major shortcoming of most research studies on black families is their a-historical character. Too many of these studies are static and examine black families at one point in time for a short time span and fail to place contemporary family situations in a historical context. Almost a century ago, at the meeting of the American Academy of Political and Social Science, W. E. B. Du Bois (1898) recommended that social scientists use a holistic framework with strong historical foundations for studying black people:

> [We]. . . .should seek to know and measure carefully all the forces and conditions that go to make up these different problems, to trace the historical development of these conditions and discover as far as possible the probable trend of further development.

Without doubt this would be difficult work, and it can with much truth be objected that we cannot ascertain, by the methods of sociological research known to us, all such facts thoroughly and accurately. To this objection it is only necessary to answer that however difficult it may be to know all about the Negro, it is certain that we can know vastly more than we do and that we can have our knowledge in more systematic and intelligible form. As things are, our opinions upon the Negro are more matters of faith than of knowledge. . . .

> [The past] work done has been lamentably unsystematic and
> fragmentary. Scientific work must be subdivided, but conclusions
> which affect the whole subject must be based on a study of the whole.
> One cannot study the Negro in freedom and come to general
> conclusions about his destiny without knowing his history in slavery.
> A vast set of problems having a common centre must, too, be studied
> according to some general plan, if the work of different students is
> to be compared or to go toward building a unified body of
> knowledge. (Du Bois 1898, 10, 12)

Du Bois argued that a proper understanding of blacks in America could not be achieved without systematically assessing the influence of historical, cultural, social, economic, and political forces. Such a holistic and balanced treatment of black families is evident in his two pioneering studies *The Philadelphia Negro* (1899) and *The Negro American Family* (1909). This comprehensive perspective was also reflected in the breadth and depth of the issues covered in the annual monographs on the "state" of black Americans published as the Atlanta University Publications Series between 1896 and 1917. Unfortunately, Du Bois's recommendation to incorporate a holistic framework in studies of black individuals and families has not been heeded by mainstream social scientists.

Nevertheless, historians and other social scientists have enhanced our understanding about black families by employing a historical perspective. The exhaustive studies by Herbert Gutman (1976) and others (Blassingame 1973; Horton and Horton 1979: Berry and Blassingame 1982) of census and other archival data and records about the family structures of black families between 1850 and 1925 strongly contested the popular "slavery destroyed the black family" thesis. Gutman's (1976) data revealed that immediately after slavery urban and rural black families had very high proportions of two-parent families that often ranged between 80 and 90 percent.

Moreover, Elizabeth Pleck's (1979) comprehensive summary of various historical studies from 1838 through 1925 revealed that the trends in female-headed families among blacks in various northern and southern cities have been cyclical, not linear. In fact, the cumulative effects of punitive laws, selective criminal prosecution, and continual racial attacks and pogroms should not make high rates of single-parent families among free blacks surprising (Curry

1981; McIntyre 1992; Horton 1993). According to Pleck's analysis, there was no glorious past period when the rate of black female-headed families was very low and then continued to rise linearly to their exceedingly high rates over the past two decades. She also found that, prior to 1925, the rates of female-headed families tended to be higher in southern cities than in northern cities:

> In fact, the female-headed household was more the product of the southern than the northern city. This conclusion can be reached by contrasting the rate of such households in northern and southern cities. Several northern cities exhibited the southern tendency toward high rates of female-headed households, but, on the average, the number of female-headed households in northern cities between 1838 and 1920 was about 25%, compared with 34% in southern cities. (Pleck 1979, 182)

However, Pleck's results are more strongly reinforced when one includes findings from one of the earliest censuses with black family data--the 1830 census. Carter G. Woodson was concerned that almost all discussions of blacks during the antebellum period refer to blacks in slavery and totally ignore the fact that more than one-tenth of all blacks were free. Since there were very few in-depth studies of the characteristics of free blacks, Woodson (1925) published the 1830 census data on all free black households in the U.S. Interestingly, this census not only had data on the number of persons in each household it also distinguished whether the head of each household was male or female. In **table 1**, we present our calculations of the proportions of black households--with two or more persons--that were headed by women in the 1830 census for selected cities and incorporate them with data compiled by Pleck and other scholars.

The data in **table 1** reveal that the rates of female-headed black families were cyclical between 1830 and 1925. For example, in Boston, the proportion of female-headed families fell from 25 to 16 percent between 1850 and 1860 and then rose to 26 percent by 1870. In Pittsburgh, the proportion of female-headed families rose from 13 to 21 percent between 1850 and 1860 and then fell to 15 percent by 1880.

However, the data in 1830 reveal much higher rates of female-headed families among free blacks in southern than in northern cities. For example, Richmond, New Orleans, and Charleston had rates of female-headed families between 55 and 65 percent, while Boston, New York, and Philadelphia had rates between 11 and 23 percent. E. Franklin Frazier's analysis (1932) of free black families in 1830 also underscores the high levels of female-headed families among southern families:

> A striking fact about these 32 (free black) families (in Augusta, Georgia in 1830) was that a woman was the head in 20 (or 62% of the) cases. . . .When we consider the large number of families with female heads in relation to the fact that in 1860 there were 325 mulattoes among the 490 free Negroes enumerated for this county, it does not seem unreasonable to conclude that in many cases white men were the fathers of the children. (Frazier 1932, 25-26)

Frazier concluded that the higher levels of female-headed families among free black families in southern than northern cities was caused by a disproportionate number of mulatto children fathered by white men. It is interesting that these high levels of female-headed families in southern cities declined sharply in subsequent decades. For example, John Blassingame (1973) concludes that by 1880, about 20 percent of the black families in New Orleans were headed by women.

Yet, when one examines the data in **table 2**, there does tend to be a linear relationship in the growth of female-headed black families between 1930 and 1990. Nevertheless, it is important to note that the proportion of black female-headed families in the U.S. rose from 19 to 23 percent between 1930 and 1940, and then declined to 18 percent by 1950 (Ricketts 1989). It appears that the devastating effects of the Great Depression of the 1930s may have contributed to the rise in one-parent black families between 1930 and 1940.

Many sociologists have also concluded that, historically, the rates of black children living in one-parent families have been much higher than white children (Furstenberg et al. 1975; Morgan et al. 1993; McDaniel 1994). For example, an in-depth analysis by Steven Ruggles (1994) of data from censuses between 1880 and 1960 revealed that black children were two to three times more likely to

**Table 1:  Proportion of Black Female-Headed Families In Selected Cities, 1830-1925**

| CITIES | 1830* | 1850 | 1860 | 1870 | 1880 | 1896 | 1905 | 1925 |
|---|---|---|---|---|---|---|---|---|
| *Total U. S.* | --- | --- | --- | --- | --- | --- | --- | --- |
| *EAST* | | | | | | | | |
| Boston | 14% | 25% | 16% | 26% | 24% | --- | --- | --- |
| Brooklyn | 11% | 33% | --- | --- | --- | --- | --- | --- |
| New York | 18% | --- | 39% | --- | --- | --- | 33% | 30% |
| Buffalo | --- | --- | --- | --- | --- | --- | 39% | 14% |
| Philadelphia | 23% | 23% | --- | --- | 26% | --- | --- | --- |
| Pittsburgh | 20% | 13% | 21% | 6% | 15% | --- | --- | --- |
| *SOUTH* | | | | | | | | |
| Baltimore | 23% | --- | --- | 23% | 46% | --- | --- | --- |
| Wash. DC. | 39% | 31% | 30% | 17% | 11% | --- | --- | --- |
| Richmond | 56% | --- | --- | --- | 34% | --- | --- | --- |
| Charleston | 65% | --- | 61% | --- | --- | --- | --- | --- |
| New Orleans | 55% | --- | --- | --- | 20% | --- | --- | --- |
| Mobile | --- | --- | 44% | --- | 34% | --- | --- | --- |
| Atlanta | --- | --- | --- | 27% | 23% | 28% | --- | --- |
| Nashville | --- | --- | --- | --- | --- | 17% | --- | --- |
| *MIDWEST* | | | | | | | | |
| Cincinnati | 11% | 21% | 26% | 22% | 21% | --- | --- | --- |
| Cleveland | --- | 7% | 17% | 15% | 16% | --- | --- | --- |
| Louisville | 27% | 34% | 33% | 20% | 23% | --- | --- | --- |

*Figures in this column were calculated by Robert B. Hill from 1830 census data in Woodson (1925).

Source:   Woodson (1925); Pleck (1979); Powell (1980); Blassingame (1973); and Harris (1976).

reside without one or both parents than were white children. While different factors may explain the cyclical rates of single-parent black families during the 19th and 20th centuries, it is evident that their higher levels relative to whites are not a recent phenomenon, as studies by Frazier (1926; 1931; 1939) also reveal. Additionally, as Gilbert Osofksy (1968) observes, the concentration of blacks in racial enclaves or "ghettos" also has a long history.

Although black families have had disproportionately high levels of female-headed families during the 19th and 20th centuries, Stephanie Coontz (1992) and other scholars caution that it should not be assumed that these families were "broken" or "disorganized." In fact, many of the single-parent black families in the past also had cultural strengths. For example, Frazier (1932; 1957: 76-79) observes that, despite the high levels of single-parent families, some of the largest numbers of middle and upper class free blacks were in Charleston and New Orleans. James Hagy (1987) also points out that many free black women in Charleston owned businesses, and Berry and Blassingame (1982) concluded that the free black antebellum community contributed to the legacy of strong black families:

> One of the most important sources of black family tradition was the antebellum free Negro community. Although haunted by poverty, the free black family was nevertheless strong. It was especially crucial in the socialization of children. Black children imbibed important lessons from their parents. As industrious and earnest Christians, parents stressed morality, the value of labor and education, and racial uplift. They held family devotional services and regularly took their children to church. If they were skilled craftsmen, they taught their trade to their sons. If not, blacks boys were frequently apprenticed to black or white artisans. Finally, and most important, black parents exemplified, in their own lives, the character traits they wanted their children to learn. (Berry and Blassingame 1982, 76)

It is important to realize that whether a family is disorganized or not depends primarily on the quality of its functioning, not on its structure. In his studies, Frazier was careful not to equate single-parent families with disorganization:

**Table 2:** **Proportion of Black Female-Headed Families In Selected Cities, 1930-1990**

| CITIES | 1930 | 1940 | 1950 | 1960 | 1970 | 1980 | 1990 |
|---|---|---|---|---|---|---|---|
| Total U.S.* | 19% | 23% | 18% | 22% | 28% | 38% | 43% |
| *EAST* | | | | | | | |
| Boston | --- | 32% | 17% | 25% | 39% | 49% | 51% |
| Brooklyn | 20% | 28% | --- | 25% | 29% | 46% | 49% |
| New York | --- | 25% | 24% | 25% | 32% | 45% | 48% |
| Buffalo | 13% | --- | 19% | 21% | 34% | 49% | 55% |
| Philadelphia | --- | 23% | 23% | 23% | 32% | 45% | 50% |
| Pittsburgh | --- | 29% | 20% | 21% | 34% | 48% | 58% |
| *SOUTH* | | | | | | | |
| Baltimore | --- | 30% | 21% | 21% | 41% | 46% | 53% |
| Wash. DC. | --- | 29% | 19% | 21% | 28% | 43% | 49% |
| Richmond | --- | --- | 25% | 23% | 32% | 44% | 50% |
| Charleston | --- | --- | --- | --- | --- | 44% | 48% |
| New Orleans | --- | 32% | 22% | 24% | 31% | 42% | 51% |
| Mobile | --- | --- | 25% | --- | 29% | 39% | 49% |
| Atlanta | --- | --- | 22% | 25% | 30% | 46% | 53% |
| Nashville | --- | --- | 25% | --- | 28% | 39% | 48% |
| *MIDWEST* | | | | | | | |
| Cincinnati | --- | 29% | 20% | 22% | 31% | 46% | 56% |
| Louisville | --- | 31% | 18% | 22% | 32% | 48% | 52% |
| Detroit | --- | 17% | 14% | 19% | 26% | 42% | 52% |
| Chicago | --- | 27% | 19% | 22% | 29% | 45% | 52% |

*Figures from 1930 to 1980 in the row for the Total U.S. are from Ricketts (1989).

Source: Ricketts (1989) and U.S. census data from 1930 to 1990.

> Some families in "delinquency areas" manage to maintain their stability and organization and exercise discipline over their children. It appears that the delinquents come not from "broken homes" (for example, "broken" by the absence of a parent) but from *disorganized* families. (Frazier 1950, 275)
>
>   Thus it has been the grandmother who has held the generations together when fathers and mothers abandoned their offspring... The Negro grandmother has not ceased to watch over the destiny of the Negro families as they have moved in ever increasing numbers to the cities during the present century....However, figures cannot give us any conception of the grandmother, unawed and still with her ancient dignity, watching over her children in the strange world of the city. (Frazier 1966, 113, 123)

Many other scholars (Reissman 1964; Lewis 1967; Valentine 1968; Ladner 1971: Kellam et al. 1982; Harrison et al. 1990; Sandven and Resnick 1990) have identified adaptive socialization strategies and other strengths among low-income female-headed black families. James Borchert (1980) conducted an in-depth study of positive adaptations and coping processes among poor single-parent and two-parent black families that lived in alley houses in Washington, D.C. between 1850 and 1970. It should be noted that the blacks who lived in alley houses in such cities as Washington, D.C., Baltimore, Philadelphia, and New York City, were considered to be members of the black "lower class" (or underclass) of that period (Du Bois 1898; Brown 1937; Groves 1974). Many antebellum black communities, such as Weeksville in Brooklyn, New York, established self-help institutions, including churches, schools, homes for the aged, orphanages, and small businesses (Maynard and Cottman 1983). Yet the pioneering ethnographic child-rearing studies by Hylan Lewis (1967) also identify many positive functioning patterns among low-income blacks in Washington, D.C. during the early 1960s.

Coontz (1992) also underscores the enduring significance of black family strengths:

> But these alternative family forms and gender roles were hardly "pathological" or "disorganized." They were part of a rich extended kin and community life. In nineteenth century Washington, D.C., for example, black working people supported more than one hundred

associations, while poor alley residents developed vibrant and cohesive community networks. Studies of many cities in the nineteenth and twentieth centuries reveal that African-American families maintained tighter and more supportive kin ties than did other urban families, taking care of elders, paupers, and orphans within family networks rather than institutionalizing them as frequently as other groups did. (Coontz 1992, 241)

Joe William Trotter (1993) underscores the importance of an historical context for enhancing our understanding of the persistence of an "underclass" in black communities:

Between 1965, the year of the controversial Moynihan Report, and 1980, out-of-wedlock black births increased from 25 to 57 percent; black female-headed families rose from 25 to 43 percent; and violent crimes and unemployment likewise increased. Still, such urban problems were not entirely new. They characterized black life in the past. By linking the growth of the urban underclass to developments of the last two decades, social science and policy studies provide inadequate insights into the historical development of the black community, its changing class structure, and the roots of urban black poverty. A historical examination of these issues reveals more connections between the past and present than much of the current literature on the urban underclass suggests. Only by bringing systematic historical analyses to the contemporary underclass debate will we be able to fully understand the changing dimensions of urban poverty. (Trotter 1993, 57)

Andrew Miller (1993) recounts the historical tendency of the American public and scholars to focus on black disorganization at periods when family instability has risen for whites:

There is also evidence that concern with "deviant" family structures is connected to a certain level of racial scapegoating and displacement. African Americans have always had significantly higher rates of female headship and teenage and extramarital births. Concern about these issues, however, has only come when such rates begin to rise significantly for whites. Thus, the Depression brought forth Frazier's early concern with matriarchy when male economic roles in the family were threatened for all Americans. The rapidly rising divorce rates in the 1960's raised Moynihan's similar concerns that a "tangle of pathology" was emerging from female headship. More recently, as teenage and unwed births have been dropping for African Americans but skyrocketing among whites, a new hysteria has arisen, which has once again been displaced onto the consistently higher, but declining, rates for African Americans. (Miller 1993, 267)

## ECOLOGICAL PERSPECTIVE

Our solutions framework also incorporates an ecological perspective, that is, an approach that permits the examination of the positive and negative effects of factors at the societal, community, family, and individual levels on the structure and functioning of African American families.  This is, therefore, a multi-disciplinary perspective, including such fields as sociology, psychology, political science, history, and economics.

Although E. Franklin Frazier's studies have often been depicted as focusing on the negative attributes of black family life, a careful examination of his works reveals a more balanced treatment.  He never succumbed, for example, to the conventional approach of treating symptoms (such as female-headed family structures) as the causes of the ills (such as poverty, unemployment, out-of-wedlock births, etc.) that afflict many African American families.

More importantly, he always employed an ecological framework that identified the impact of external forces in the large society on the structure and functioning of black families.  In fact, contrary to the deficit model, Frazier's analyses consistently attributed the primary sources of family instability to external forces (racism, urbanization, technological changes, recessionary cycles, etc.), and not to factors internal to the black family.

Frazier's (1957) ecological studies of the black communities in Chicago and New York reveal that the structure, functioning and class status of black families varied according to their proximity to the central business district of those cities. To support his thesis that the growth of the black community corresponded to the growth of the city, Frazier applied Park's theory of ecological zones.  In Chicago, he identified seven zones, in which the poorest families were disproportionately located in Zones I and II (which were closest to the city's center and had the highest concentrations of factories and other industrial establishments).  The largest number of high income and two-parent families were located in Zones VI and VII (which were equivalent to "suburban" residential areas).

Frazier's ecological approach helped to explain the high rates of family disorganization (such as illegitimacy, juvenile delinquency, crime, female-headed families, etc.) among blacks as a result of selection and segregation processes in cities that spatially distributed groups in sections of communities based on such factors as recency of migration, racial and ethnic group, poverty, education and illiteracy, occupation, etc. Frazier (1931) notes that the sections of Chicago that had high rates of delinquency among blacks were the same areas that had high rates of delinquency when European immigrants lived there.

One of the most significant efforts to marry Du Bois's holistic framework to Frazier's ecological approach for studying black families was undertaken by Billingsley (1968). Based on the structural-functional theory of the family posited by Talcott Parsons and Robert Bales (1955), Billingsley employed an ecological framework that characterized black families as a social subsystem mutually interacting with subsystems in the black community and with subsystems in the wider (white) society.

Schematically, black families were depicted by a circle embedded within a larger circle that symbolized the black community, which, in turn, was embedded within a larger circle that symbolized the wider society. To adequately understand black families, Billingsley's systems model requires examining the separate and combined effects on family functioning of: (a) Internal subsystems in families, such as intra-household interactions involving husbands and wives, parents and children, siblings, other relatives, and nonrelatives; (b) External subsystems in the black community, such as schools, churches, peer groups, social clubs, black businesses, neighborhood associations, and other community-based groups; (c) External subsystems in the wider society, such as societal forces and institutional policies in the areas of economics, technology, politics, education, health, welfare, law, culture, religion, and the media.

In his later work, Billingsley (1992) placed greater emphasis on the reciprocal interactions between family subsystems and external subsystems in order to avoid the mistaken assumption that the relation was unidirectional, that is, from external subsystems to family subsystems.  Billingsley's formulation was one of several efforts by social scientists to use ecological or systems frameworks for examining family functioning.  Orville Brim (1957) offered a social systems approach for assessing patterns of child development, and a comprehensive literature review by Reuben Hill and Donald Hansen (1960) highlighted several studies that used a systems perspective to examine American families.  Urie Bronfenbrenner (1979) also advocated the use of ecological frameworks for studying child and family development.  However, Billingsley was the first scholar to adapt the ecological/systems framework explicitly for the study of black family life.

To broaden the perspective of black family research from its traditional male-headed/female-headed dichotomy, Billingsley (1968) systematically identified the structural diversity of black families by developing a typology depicting thirty-two different kinds of nuclear, extended and augmented family households.  This typology underscores the fact that the structure, functioning, and needs of black families may change significantly as family members pass through various stages of their life cycles.  Unfortunately, the important research and policy implications of Billingsley's systems framework and family typology have not been incorporated by most black family researchers (Williams and Stockton 1973; Payton 1982).

Walter Allen (1978b) evaluated the relative merits of several conceptual frameworks for studying black families.  He felt that a major weakness of the structural-functional systems model was its static character.  Thus, he urged that developmental concepts be incorporated into the ecological/systems framework.

Allen contends that the developmental approach was dynamic, because it viewed families and family members as moving through a life cycle characterized by a series of developmental stages.  At each stage of the life cycle, families (due to compositional, positional, and individual changes) are confronted with different demands and varying resources to meet those demands.  On the other hand, he thought the systems paradigm was more effective in linking family members to the demands and resources of external subsystems in the black community and in the wider society.  Thus, Allen felt that both approaches--ecological/systems and developmental--should be employed to enhance the quality of black family studies. Margaret Spencer (1990) and other scholars have incorporated the developmental and ecological frameworks for studying black families in their works.

Another ecological perspective that many scholars have found useful in studying black families is Robert K. Merton's theory of anomie and deviance, which is also popularly known as the blocked opportunity thesis (Willie 1976; Bowman and Howard 1985). Merton (1957) asserts that high rates of deviant behavior are expected among groups in American society who are faced with class or racial barriers that impede the achievement of societal goals through legitimate means (such as education and employment). Thus, such disadvantaged groups are likely to be highly concentrated among four deviant role types: innovation, ritualism, retreatism, and rebellion. Retreatists and rebels withdraw from attaining societal goals; innovators use alternative strategies to achieve them. Our work places special attention on the innovative strategies that black families employ to achieve upward mobility for adults as well as for their children against overwhelming odds.

In a subsequent work, Merton (1964) expanded on his original formulation by offering an ecological framework that requires assessing the separate and combined effects of factors at the societal, community, group, and individual levels on rates of deviant or conforming behavior among various groups in society (Hill, 1980). Clearly, Merton's blocked opportunity thesis enhances our understanding of the range of adaptations made by black families in response to community and societal factors when it is synthesized with Billingsley's systems framework, Du Bois's holistic perspective, Frazier's ecological framework, and Allen's developmental approach.

## CULTURAL PERSPECTIVE

Many scholars (Nobles 1974, 1981; Sudarkasa 1975, 1980; Harvey 1985; Wilson 1986; McDaniel 1990) have emphasized the importance of the African cultural heritage for understanding the functioning of contemporary African American families. Wade Nobles (1974) has underscored the "Africanity" of black families:

> Furthermore, the black family, we contend, can only be understood as a unit or system deriving its primary characteristics, form and definition from its African nature. . . .
>   It is, therefore, suggested that what determines the special form black families take and the unique relational patterns expressed by black families is primarily the sense of Africanity or being in tune with or responsive to an African world-view or sense of the universe. (Nobles 1974, 11)

Martin and Martin (1995) use both historical and cultural perspectives to provide a foundation for social work knowledge that is rooted in the black experience. They adroitly use the concepts of "moaning," "mourning," and "morning," to describe the progression of the black experience from problem identification, and healing processes to problem-solving. The works of Maulana Karenga (1982, 1986) have also made a persuasive case for placing analyses of black families within a cultural framework.  For example, Karenga (1986) contends:

> Culture is key to understanding and solving the crisis in the black community and family. . . .We must totalize the approach and that means taking a cultural approach.  This approach not only includes stress on social ethics, but offers critique and correctives in the seven basic areas of culture--religion, history, social organization, economic organization, political organization, creative production (i.e, art, music, and literature), and ethos--the collective self-consciousness achieved as a result of antiquity in the other six areas. (Karenga 1986, 51)

One of the most enduring contributions that Maulana Karenga made to pay homage to the African legacy was the creation of Kwanza as an African American holiday in 1965.  Kwanzaa, which is commemorated from 26 December - 1 January, comprises daily celebrations that focus on each of the seven principles of the *Nguzo Saba*:
  1. *Umoja* (unity): to strive for and maintain unity in the family, community, nation, and race.
  2. *Kujichagulia* (self-determination): to define ourselves, name ourselves, and speak for ourselves instead of being defined, named, created for, and spoken for by others.

3. *Ujima* (collective work and responsibility): to build and maintain our own community, to make our sisters' and brothers' problems our problems and to solve them together.

4. *Ujamaa* (cooperative economics): to build and maintain our own stores, shops, and other businesses and to profit from them together.

5. *Nia* (purpose): to make our collective vocation the building and developing of our community in order to restore our people to their traditional greatness.

6. *Kuumba* (creativity): to do always as much as we can, in the way we can, in order to leave our community more beautiful and beneficial than we inherited it.

7. *Imani* (faith): to believe with all our heart in our people, our parents, our teachers, our leaders and the righteousness and victory of our struggle.

## PROBLEM IDENTIFICATION

Any solutions framework must include the identification of the major problems and challenges that affect the structure and functioning of African American families. Black scholars who focus on black family strengths must heed the warning of Joseph White and Thomas Parham (1990) not to avoid examination of their weaknesses:

> While our reactions (to negative descriptions of black families) have succeeded in serving as a critique of poor scholarship, by implication, some of our reactions have also clouded the fact that a specific phenomenon observed exists in reality. The result is that many of us in the Black community ignore social pathology in our families and communities, believing instead that "since White folks said it, it must not be true." Consequently, we exert little effort in trying to address the issues that need correcting. (White and Parham 1990, 33)

Over the past two decades, increasing numbers of black families have experienced rising levels of unemployment, poverty, divorce, separation, out-of-wedlock births, crime, delinquency, spousal abuse, child abuse, alcoholism, drug abuse, poor health, and AIDS.

We shall now provide a brief overview of recent economic and social instability among African American families.

**Economic Instability**

After making unprecedented strides in the 1960s, black families experienced severe social and economic setbacks during the 1970s and 1980s. A sharp rise in unemployment caused by back-to-back recessions was a major obstacle. In the years 1970-90, this nation experienced five recessions--1970-71, 1974-75, 1980, 1981-82 and 1990-91. Before blacks were able to recover from one slump, they were hit by another one. Consequently, unemployment among all blacks soared from 6 to 20 percent between 1969 and 1983. Although unemployment also rose sharply among whites during this period, unlike blacks, their post-recession jobless rates returned to their lower pre-recession levels.

The sharp increase in economic instability led directly to family instability. Over that 14-yr period, the proportion of black families headed by women increased from 28 to 42 percent. During the years 1970-83, every one percent increase in black unemployment was correlated with a one percent rise in single-parent families. Many studies have found that economic forces, such as recessions, have devastating social consequences. According to Mary Merva and Richard Fowles (1992), the 1990-91 recession was responsible for 224,000 property crimes, 63,000 violence crimes, 38,000 fatal heart attacks and strokes, and 1,500 homicides.

Yet, it is important to point out that these official unemployment figures sharply understate the actual level of joblessness in the African American community. Large numbers of blacks who are "discouraged workers" (that is, they want work but have given up actively seeking it) are left out of the Labor Department figures. When these workers are added, the jobless rates double. The official jobless rate for blacks was 11.3 percent in 1990, but according to the National Urban League's Hidden Unemployment Index, the actual unemployment rate among blacks was 21.5 percent--about twice as high. It should be noted that the highest level of unemployment for all workers during the Great Depression of the 1930s was 25 percent. Thus, it is no exaggeration to assert that joblessness in the black community over the past two decades has been at Great Depression levels.

Black youth are also disproportionately affected by high levels of unemployment. Although the official jobless rates for black youth was 31.1 percent in 1990, their hidden unemployment rate was 53.1 percent. Thus, one out of every two black youth who want work cannot obtain it. Such alarming jobless rates among black youth are important contributors to high levels of crime, delinquency, and drug trafficking, especially in inner-cities. Rising levels of unemployment among black families led to a widening of the income gap with whites. In 1970, black families had a median income ($6,279) that was 61 percent of white family median income ($10,236). By 1990, the ratio of black family income ($21,423) to white family income ($36,915) fell to 58 percent.

The decline in the black-to-white income ratio is partly accounted for by the sharp rise in multiple earners among white families and a sharp decline in number of workers among black families. Historically, black families had a higher proportion of two earners than white families. During the 1970s and 1980s, however, there was a reversal of this pattern. While the proportion of black families with two or more earners fell steeply from 54 to 46 percent between 1970 and 1990, the proportion of white families with two or more earners rose from 53 to 60 percent.

Rising levels of black unemployment led to a sharp increase in poverty during the 1970s and 1980s. The number of poor black families increased by 700,000 between 1969 and 1989, but their poverty rate remained at about three out of ten over the twenty-year period. Interestingly, although the number of black female-headed families in poverty increased by 800,000, their poverty rate declined from 54 to 48 percent. However, the sharpest increases in poverty occurred among black children. The number of black children in poverty increased by 500,000, and their poverty rate rose from 42 to 44 percent. It should also be noted that the number of poor white children also rose sharply over the past two decades.

Despite such increases in economic deprivation, it is important to note that the proportion of black families on welfare increased during the 1970s, but decreased during the 1980s. While the proportion of black families on welfare rose from 18 to 24 percent between 1969 and 1979, the proportion fell to 21 percent by 1989. Thus, contrary to popular beliefs about widespread dependency, eight out of ten (79 percent) black families currently do not receive any public assistance. (fig. 1)

According to conventional wisdom, the sharp increases in female-headed black families are reputedly due to the easy availability of welfare. Yet, one does not find a consistent linear relationship when one correlates welfare with black female-headed families over the past two decades. Indeed, between 1969 and 1979, the proportion of black families on welfare rose (from 18 to 24 percent), while the proportion of families headed by black women also rose (from 28 to 40 percent). However, in the years 1979-89, while the proportion of black families on welfare declined (to 21 percent), the proportion of female-headed black families continued to rise (to 44 percent). Obviously, one cannot infer that welfare contributed to the rise in black female-headed families during the 1980s (See trend data in fig. 1). Moreover, many scholars (Ellwood 1988a, 1988b; Wilson 1987; Rank 1994b; Offner 1995; Moffitt 1995) have concluded that welfare could not have been a significant determinant of the formation of single-parent families during the 1970s--due to the declining purchasing power of welfare grants as a result of spiraling inflation.

A major determinant of the rise in poverty among female-headed black families was the sharp rise in unemployment. Despite their higher educational and occupational levels, black women heading families were almost three times more likely to be unemployed in 1990 (14.3 percent) than they were in 1970 (5.6 percent). Families headed by black women are disproportionately poor not because they do not have husbands but because they do not have jobs. Only three out of ten (29 percent) employed women heading black families (in 1989) are poor, compared with seven out of ten (70 percent) unemployed women heading black families.

## Social Instability

Another important source of instability among black families over the past two decades was the high levels of out-of-wedlock births. Yet, it should also be emphasized that, contrary to popular belief, out-of-wedlock birth rates among black unwed mothers 15-44

**Fig. 1:**    **Black Welfare Families Vs Black Female-headed Families, 1969-89**

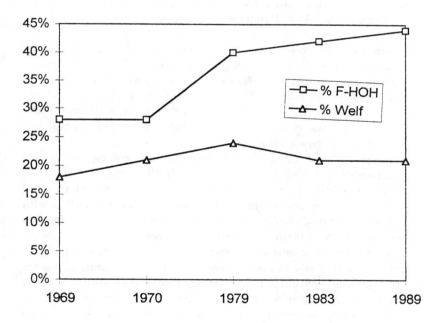

**Source:**    U.S. Census Bureau Current Population Survey data from 1969 to 1989.

years old actually *declined* sharply from 95.5 to 77.0 over the 15-year period from 1970 and 1985, while *rising* steadily from 13.9 to 22.5 among white unwed mothers. Similar trends occurred among black and white teenagers. While the out-of-wedlock birth rates among black teenagers steadily declined from 96.9 to 87.6 between 1970 and 1985, the rates among white teenagers doubled from 10.9 to 20.8. However, the out-of-wedlock birth rates among black unwed women rose to 90.5 by 1990 among black unwed women aged 15-44 years and to 106.0 by 1990 among black unwed females aged 15-19. Yet, between 1991-1994, birthrates declined among all teenagers--black and white. Nevertheless, by 1994 black teens were about three times more likely than white teens to have out-of-wedlock babies (U.S. Department of Health and Human Services 1996).

Since blacks account for almost half of the adolescent out-of-wedlock births, the social and economic viability of black families will be acutely affected. Because of inadequate health care and nutrition, babies born to black teenagers are at-risk of low-birth weight or dying in infancy. Moreover, their high dropout rates increase the risk of black teenage mothers becoming unemployed and having to go on welfare.

Although we have focused on out-of-wedlock births to adolescents, a comprehensive study by HHS (National Center for Health Statistics 1995) reveals that seven out of ten nonmarital births in the U.S. are to adult women who live alone as well as with unmarried mates. These out-of-wedlock births, which also include second and third births, are occurring increasingly among women from all socioeconomic strata and racial-ethnic groups. The HHS study also reminds us that nonmarital births contribute to higher rates of single-parent families among blacks than whites because black women are much less likely than white women to marry before conception and to relinquish their out-of-wedlock children for formal adoption.

Unprecedented levels of crime, violence, and drug abuse have also destabilized many black families. With drug trafficking rampant in most inner-cities, the easy availability of guns have led to record-level homicides. The disproportionate surge in deaths among blacks contributed to the first decline in black life expectancy since 1962. Although the life expectancy of all blacks fell from 69.7 to 69.4

between 1984 and 1986, it increased to 70.3 by 1990. Thus, between 1970 and 1990, the life expectancy among blacks increased from 64.1 to 70.3. These increases occurred among both black males and females. While the life expectancy among black males rose from 64.1 to 66.0, it rose among black females from 68.3 to 74.5.

One of the most ominous family destabilizing factors has been the disparate spread of AIDS (Acquired Immune Deficiency Syndrome) among blacks. Blacks comprised 35 percent of the 496,896 AIDS cases reported in the U.S. by 1995, and Blacks accounted for one-third (33 percent) of the 305,843 deaths from AIDS by 1995. Overall, blacks are three times more likely than whites to contract AIDS. Black females are fourteen times more likely than white females to contract AIDS. Moreover, black children, who comprise 60 percent of all children with AIDS, are fifteen times more likely than white children to contract AIDS. By the year 2000, the number of new AIDS cases among blacks is projected to exceed one million.

A proper identification of problems should attempt to distinguish secondary symptoms from primary causal factors. It should also identify causal factors at the societal, community, family, and individual levels that were major contributors to increasing economic and social instability among black families. While key societal forces include racism, sexism, demographic trends, industrialization, immigration, key social policies include urban renewal, affirmative action, fiscal policies, welfare policies, and the media. Although many of the social forces and policies had positive effects on the functioning of African American families, they also had unintended, negative consequences. We will now examine selected societal forces and social policies that have contributed to the destabilization of African American families.

## SOCIETAL FORCES

### Racism

Unfortunately, racism continues to be the predominant societal force that impedes the advancement of black families. Nevertheless, there is still much disagreement about whether racism has been declining or increasing. According to most opinion polls and surveys, there has been a decline in prejudicial attitudes or stereotypes among whites toward racial minorities (Harris and Associates 1989). Yet, even if this decline is accurate, it would only reflect the attitudes of individuals, not their actual behavior, nor the discriminatory actions of institutions.

The proponents of the declining significance of racism focus mainly on individual prejudice and fail to assess the impact of institutional racism. Accordingly, Stokely Carmichael and Charles Hamilton (1967) distinguish individual and institutional racism as follows:

> Racism is both overt and covert. It takes two, closely related forms: individual whites acting against individual blacks, and acts by the total white community against the black community. We call these individual racism and institutional racism. The first consists of overt acts by individuals which cause death, injury or the violent destruction of property. This type can be reached by television cameras; it can frequently be observed in the process of commission. The second type is less overt, far more subtle, less identifiable in terms of specific individuals committing the acts. But it is no less destructive of human life. The second type originates in the operation of established and respected forces in the society, and thus receives far less public condemnation than the first type. (Carmichael and Hamilton 1967, 4)

Moreover, according to Carmichael and Hamilton, institutional racism may also be unconscious and unintentional. Based on their definition, we have identified one important form of institutional racism--structural discrimination. We define structural discrimination as the disparate adverse effects on racial and ethnic groups of societal forces or policies, even if those actions may not have been intended to be discriminatory (Hill 1988). Such racially disparate policies often rely on non-racial proxies (such as income, residence, family structure, education, etc.) that are strongly correlated with race (Hill 1992; Pincus 1996)). The importance of unintentional racism was underscored by Downs (1970):

> Racism can occur even if the people causing it have no intention of subordinating others because of color, or are totally unaware of doing so. Admittedly, this implication is sure to be extremely controversial.

Most Americans believe racism is bad. But how can anyone be "guilty" of doing something bad when he does not realize he is doing it? Racism can be a matter of result rather than intention because many institutional structures in America that most whites do not recognize as subordinating others because of color actually injure minority group members far more than deliberate racism. (Downs 1970, 78)

We contend that structurally discriminatory societal forces and social policies have had disparate adverse impact on many African Americans and their families. For example, to protect the solvency of the Social Security Trust Fund in 1983, the 98th Congress raised the eligible age for retirement at full benefits to 67 years old by the year 2022. This policy change, although not intentionally racially discriminatory, will have differential consequences for whites and blacks, due to their different life expectancies (Hill et al. 1993).

Black males will be affected most severely, since their current life expectancy of 65 years insures that most of them will not live long enough to collect full benefits. Moreover, this increase in the eligible age for retirement benefits will have devastating effects on the families of thousands of black men and women who are forced into early retirement at reduced benefits because of ill health resulting from years of working in physically debilitating and hazardous jobs and industries.

Another example of structural discrimination are the adoption practices of child welfare agencies (Gurak et al. 1982). Many adoption agencies require potential adoptive parents to meet the following criteria: husband-wife couples, middle-income, no children of their own, and less than 45 years old. Yet, research studies (Hill 1977) reveal that the black families that are most interested in formally adopting children tend to be one-parent, low-income, with children of their own, and over 45 years old. Since such structurally discriminatory eligibility criteria screen out potential black families, hundreds of black children continue to languish in the limbo of foster care for most of their lives.

*Environmental racism*, a concept coined by Reverend Benjamin Chavis, is another example of structural discrimination. A pioneering national study, *Toxic Wastes and Race*, conducted by the Commission for Racial Justice (1987) of the United Council of

Churches revealed that inner-city black communities were selected disproportionately as sites for landfills, garbage dumps, waste disposal facilities, and incinerators. This study found race to be the most important factor in locating toxic waste sites, since blacks were over represented in the cities with the largest number of abandoned toxic waste sites, and poor black communities were much more likely to be sites than poor white communities. Other studies (Cohen 1994) have confirmed these conclusions by discovering similar racial disparities in the location of waste disposal sites. Studies conducted by Robert Bullard (1990) and other scholars reveal that families living in such communities have high symptoms and illnesses resulting from exposure to toxic chemicals at high levels.

An example of structural discrimination in the criminal justice system is the passage of congressional legislation in 1986 that instituted the 100-1 ratio that counts one gram of crack cocaine as equal to 100 grams of powder cocaine. Thus, individuals who are arrested for possessing fifty grams of crack cocaine will get a mandatory ten-year sentence, while those who possess fifty grams of powder cocaine will get a one-year sentence. Since blacks are more likely to use crack, and whites are more likely to use powder, blacks will get much longer sentences than whites--although both groups may have comparable amounts of cocaine. Moreover, because similar amounts of both powder and crack have the same destructive effects, one would think they should have equal federal penalties. It is clear why many black leaders characterize this structurally discriminatory legislation as institutional racism (Cauchon 1993, 10-A).

**Sexism**

Sexism, the subordination of women, is another societal pattern that has a negative impact on black families (Harley and Terborg-Penn 1978; Rodgers-Rose 1980). Although white women encounter sexism, they do not experience racism. Moreover, because large numbers of black women head families, they are likely to experience both gender and racial discrimination in employment, housing, banking, health, adoption, foster care, social welfare, and the administration of justice. Diana Pearce and Harriette McAdoo

(1981) underscore several sex-specific reasons for the increased feminization of poverty:

[W]omen, especially minority women, may be poor for some of the same reasons as men, but few men become poor because of female causes. Men generally do not become poor because of divorce, sex-role socialization, sexism or, of course, pregnancy. Indeed, some may lift themselves out of poverty by the same means that plunge women into it. The same divorce rate that frees a man from the financial burdens of a family may result in poverty for his ex-wife and children. Distinct reasons for the poverty among women can be traced back to two sources. First, in American culture women continue to carry the major burden of childbearing. This sex-role socialization has many ramifications. For example, women tend to make career choices that anticipate that they will interrupt their participation in the labor force to bear children. The second major source of poverty is the limited opportunities available to women in the labor market. Occupational segregation, sex discrimination, and sexual harassment combine to limit both income and mobility for women workers. (Pearce and McAdoo 1981, 17)

According to Robert Staples and Leanor Johnson (1993), black women not only receive sexist treatment from white males but from black men as well:

Most men are conditioned through the socialization process to believe that they are endowed with qualities of leadership and that women should play a subordinate role in human affairs. Black men cannot help but be affected by the stereotyped roles of men and women. To some degree, they internalize the same values of male supremacy that White men do. (Staples and Johnson 1993, 128)
. . .To further refute the notion of a castrated Black male, Hooks (1981) raises the issue of Black male sexism. She contends that male superiority is an institutional value into which Black men are also socialized. While Black men are denied many of the ordinary perquisites of manhood, they are still elevated above the status of Black women on the basis of gender affiliation alone. Using the statements of certain Black male leaders, she advances the argument that Black women must not allow Black men to define the role of women as subordinate and unequal. The conclusion is that Black women should hold their men accountable for their actions and

demand parity in decision-making and leadership organization. (Staples and Johnson 1993, 133)

## Demographic Trends

Key demographic trends include fertility patterns and the declining marriage rates among blacks. The structure and functioning of black families during the 1970s and 1980s were affected markedly by the baby boom cohort, that is, the record-level surge in birth rates in the United States after World War II. During the first half of the 1970s, the number of adolescents between the ages of 16 and 19 reached record levels. However, during the same period, the number of children born to married women declined sharply, while the number born to unmarried women fell more slowly. Thus, these demographic shifts led to alarming increases in the number of out-of-wedlock births to adolescents among whites as well as blacks.

As the baby boom cohort reached adulthood by the 1980s, the proportion of out-of-wedlock births to teenagers steadily declined. Nevertheless, since black teenagers are three times more likely than white teenagers to have out-of-wedlock babies, adolescent pregnancy continues to be a major contributor to black family instability. However, since 90 percent of black unwed teen mothers continued to live with their parents, adolescent parents were not the main reason for the surge in female-headed black families since the 1970s.

Delayed marriage, low rates of remarriage, and singlehood have contributed markedly to the formation of single-parent black families. Although marriage rates also declined among whites, they have fallen more sharply among blacks. In order to assess systematically the extent to which various social and economic factors contribute to the disproportionate decline in marriage rates among African Americans, M. Belinda Tucker and Claudia Mitchell-Kernan commissioned an interdisciplinary group of scholars to prepare papers on related topics. The research findings of this group were compiled in an engrossing volume entitled *The Decline in Marriage Among African Americans,* which was edited by Tucker and Mitchell-Kernan (1995).

Most of the scholars found little evidence that the availability of welfare was an important contributor to the rise in female-headed blacks families during the 1970s and 1980s. On the other hand, the sex ratios among blacks--the lower availability of marriageable males to females--were more important factors in accounting for the low marriage (and remarriage) rates and the formation of single-parent families among blacks. The editors concluded that most of these studies revealed that sex ratios, when combined with economic factors (especially male employment), had the strongest effects on the decline in marriage rates and the increase in female-headed families among blacks.

Among persons of all ages, there are only 90 black men to 100 black women, while there are 95 white men to 100 white women. Interestingly, under the age of 15, black males outnumber black females, but among persons 25-44 years old, there are only 87 black men for every 100 black women, while there are about equal numbers of white men and white women in that age category. However, when one corrects for the disproportionate census undercount of black men, the gap narrows markedly to about 95 black men for every 100 black women between the ages of 25 and 44. Yet, a shortage of marriageable black men continues to exist because of a number of factors: high rates of unemployment, underemployment, arrest records, incarceration, disability, drug addiction, homicide and suicides. Stewart and Scott (1978) attribute the unavailability of marriageable black males to "institutional decimation," the disproportionate marginalization of black men from productive sectors of the society by institutional forces and processes (Darity and Myers 1995).

**Industrialization**

Major industrial and technological changes have had significant effects on black families. Industrialization brought about structural transformations in the American economy and had both positive and negative consequences. It gradually shifted economic emphasis from agriculture to manufacturing, and then from manufacturing to services. In this process, technology has shifted from low-tech to high-tech, or from labor-intensive to capital-intensive production. Its impact on employment sectors has been a shift from the public to the private sector, and in occupations, from farm to factory work, factory to office, and from self-employed to salaried (Bluestone and Harrison 1982; Drake and Cayton 1945).

Frazier (1931) describes at length how the shift from an agricultural to a manufacturing economy had destabilizing effects on rural black families between 1865 and 1925. Drake and Cayton (1945) provide an in-depth analysis of how specific industrial changes undermined the economic well-being of blacks between World War I and II. Several scholars (Glasgow 1981; Wilson 1987) have identified current technological change as a key source of disadvantage for blacks with respect to education and technical skills.

On the other hand, industrialization has also had many positive effects, especially in raising the occupational and earnings levels of wage-earners in black families as they moved from farm to factory work, or from lower-paying operative jobs to higher-paying clerical and technical jobs (Frazier 1949).

The exodus of jobs from central cities during the 1960s and 1970s to suburban communities and abroad was a major factor in the sharp increase in unemployment among inner-city black workers and in the destabilization of their families. The changeover in the economy from manufacturing jobs with middle-income salaries to low-income service jobs markedly undermined the ability of working-class parents to provide for their family's needs (Bluestone and Harrison 1982; Wilson 1987; Wilson 1996).

**Immigration**

Immigration has had many adverse effects on black families. During slavery, employment opportunities for free blacks in the North were directly related to competition for those jobs from newly-arriving foreigners (Frazier 1949). An analysis conducted by Charles Johnson (1930) revealed that between 1880-1920, black migration to the North was highest when foreign immigration to the U. S. was lowest, and was lowest when foreign immigration was at its peak (fig. 2).

After emancipation, numerous race riots broke out between immigrants and blacks over perceived or actual job competition. Immigrants also adopted restrictive labor union practices in order to eliminate blacks from certain jobs and industries (Drake and

**Fig. 2:  European Immigration Vs. Negro Migration, 1880-1920**

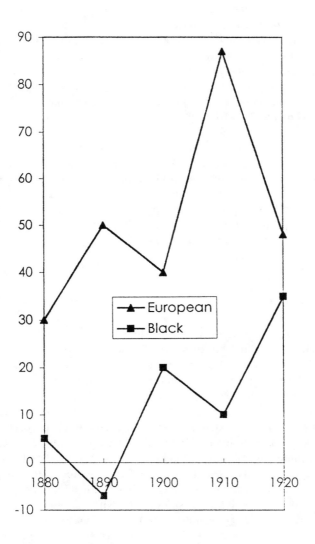

Source:     Johnson (1930).

Cayton 1945). Consequently, blacks made their greatest occupational advances during the World Wars, when European immigration was curtailed.

Recent studies suggest that an increasing source of black unemployment is competition from Hispanic and Asian immigrants--legal and illegal. Between 1975 and 1980, Hispanics obtained the same number of new jobs as blacks, although the Hispanic population was only about half the size of the black population. Asians obtained about half as many of the new jobs created during that period as blacks, although the number of Asians was only one-fifth the size of the black population (Hill 1981). Moreover, an analysis by James Stewart and T. J. Hyclak (1986) revealed that immigrants--other than those from Cuba or the West Indies--adversely affected the earnings of black men in central cities. Since most demographers predict that Asians and Hispanics will constitute the fastest-growing groups in the U.S. into the twenty-first century, job competition between them and blacks is likely to become more acute in the near future.

## SOCIAL POLICIES

### Urban Renewal

Urban renewal and other slum clearance policies had mixed consequences for black families. On the one hand, blacks who were relocated through slum clearance usually moved to housing facilities that were better than the substandard conditions they left. Yet, in many instances, urban renewal also destabilized black communities and families by disrupting social networks and closing numerous black businesses. Not only were blacks disproportionately dispersed to other areas but highways, bridges, and expressways divided or often completely destroyed viable black communities. The previous slum neighborhoods, which were often located in "prime" downtown locations, were then "gentrified" with middle and upper income housing for white residents or with public or private institutions, such as government buildings, universities, medical centers, etc. Examples of black communities that were gentrified include Georgetown and the South West section of Washington, D.C. and areas surrounding many universities, such as George

Washington University, the University of Chicago, the University of Illinois at Chicago, the University of Pennsylvania, etc. Because blacks comprised over 60 percent of those displaced, urban renewal became regarded among blacks as "Negro removal." However, Sigmund Shipp (1997) reminds us that urban renewal had mixed effects on the black community, since it often had positive consequences for middle-class black individuals, groups, and institutions.

It is rarely noted that slum clearance and urban renewal were major factors in the development and later transformation of public housing. As a means of fighting blight in the 1930s, the Low-Rent Public Housing (LRPH) program was established by the Housing Act of 1937 to provide affordable housing for low-income families in central cities. During the initial decade (1937-48) of public housing, blacks were only a small fraction of the residents, since such projects were originally designed for white working class immigrants. Blacks made their major inroads into public housing during its second decade (1949-59), mainly as a result of urban renewal. Thus, the proportion of blacks in public housing rose from 38 to 46 percent between 1952-61. (Newman et al. 1978; Leigh 1991). Although working poor couples were given highest priority for public housing during its first decade, thousands of nonworking poor families had to be accommodated during the second decade because of their displacement from slum areas by urban renewal. In the years 1952-74, the proportion of public housing residents who worked fell from 71 to 27 percent (Hill, 1992). To prevent displaced blacks from following whites to other sections of the cities or to the suburbs, numerous localities built high-rise public housing developments for blacks in segregated areas. Consequently, urban renewal also contributed substantially to the "hyper-segregation" of blacks in inner-city areas and the concentration of the black underclass (Massey and Denton 1993).

By the 1990s, cities, such as Baltimore and Chicago, began to demolish high-rise public housing and replace them with scattered site or low-rise housing for mixed income families. Since many of these high-rises are situated in desirable downtown locations, it is questionable whether many of the low-income families who were displaced will be able to return to those neighborhoods. It is far more likely that those former slum sites will be gentrified by major institutions, such as universities, medical centers, or office complexes.

## Affirmative Action

Affirmative action policies suffered severe setbacks during the 1990s from a succession of adverse rulings by the Supreme Court. During 1995, the Reagan-Bush Supreme Court found numerous federal and state statutes enacted to provide equal opportunities for minorities unconstitutional. These decisions were related to minority business set-asides, university scholarships for black students, and electoral redistricting. The conservative majority of the Supreme Court declared that special initiatives were no longer needed for minorities because America has virtually achieved a "color-blind" society.

There has been widespread disagreement about the impact of affirmative action. While some scholars (Jones 1981; Pinkney 1984) contend that these policies have enhanced equal opportunities for all blacks, other analysts (Wilson 1987; Glazer 1975; Loury 1984) argue that affirmative action has helped mainly middle-class blacks.

A major reason for the continuing controversy over affirmative action is the inability of proponents and critics to agree on common definitions. Conservatives characterize it as "reverse discrimination" against whites to achieve equal results for "unqualified" minorities, while liberals describe it as compensatory action for past discrimination and a means to achieve equal opportunities for "qualified" minorities. Moreover, conservatives characterize affirmative action standards as "quotas," whereas liberals see such standards as "goals" and "timetables."

Both liberals and conservatives mistakenly identify redressing past intentional discrimination as the overriding goal of affirmative action. They consequently ignore the importance of eradicating *current* individual and institutional discrimination. Many observers argue that if racism no longer exists, the effects of past racism would be minimal.

Although numerical quotas have received the most publicity, they constitute only a tiny fraction of all affirmative action remedies. The overwhelming majority of measures involve education, moral persuasion, voluntary compliance, negotiation, mediation, guidelines, and timetables. Courts have only required quotas as a last resort for employers who have failed to demonstrate good faith efforts to discontinue or redress discriminatory policies. Furthermore, little media attention has been given to the large number of affirmative action decisions and settlements that have provided back-pay to thousands of black workers who have been unjustly confined to lower paying jobs than white workers. In 1996, for example, Texaco Inc., the oil giant, agreed to an out-of-court settlement of a class-action discrimination suit by awarding $140 million to its black employees.

In fact, many studies consistently reveal that working class and poor blacks benefitted disproportionately from the educational and occupational gains over the past three decades. According to an in-depth study of occupational mobility of blacks during the 1960s by Sar Levitan, William Johnson, and Robert Taggart (1975), laborers and agricultural and domestic workers experienced more upgrading than middle-class workers. Bart Landry (1978) concluded that over 80 percent of black middle-class males in both 1962 and 1973 had moved up from poor and working class origins.

Many analysts (Jones 1981; Pinkney 1984) have revealed a declining commitment to affirmative action by universities, businesses, and government. Consequently, the proportion of black students enrolled in college has steadily declined since the mid-1970s. Other analysts (Palmer and Sawhill 1984) call attention to sharp budget cuts in government agencies responsible for enforcing affirmative action policies. Clearly, more aggressive, not less, affirmative action measures are needed.

**Fiscal and Monetary Policies**

During the 1970s, black families were disproportionately affected by federal monetary policies that induced back-to-back recessions in order to fight inflation. Thus, at the same time that black families were reeling from the effects of periodic recessions, they were also subjected to double-digit inflation. Although classical economic theory held that it was impossible to have high levels of unemployment and inflation simultaneously, the new term *stagflation* was coined. In the years 1969-80, consumer prices soared at an unprecedented annual rate of 12 percent, compared with only

3 percent during the 1960s. Each of the four presidents during that twelve-year period--Nixon, Ford, Carter and Reagan--vowed not to fight inflation on the backs of the unemployed, but the Federal Reserve Board raised interest rates so high that soaring unemployment brought on four recessions--1970-71, 1974-75, 1980, and 1981-82.

## Block Grants

Although block grants are usually omitted from most policy analyses of black families, the transformation of categorical grants to block grants during the 1970s and 1980s contributed significantly to the shift in government resources from blacks and low-income groups to middle-income groups and communities. As a result of President Nixon's "New Federalism" efforts to transfer the administration of federal social programs to states and localities, many of the social programs of the 1960s were combined into broad revenue sharing block grants. Model Cities was replaced by the Community Development Block Grant (CDBG); the Manpower Development and Training Act (MDTA) was replaced by the Comprehensive Employment and Training Act (CETA), Nixon's manpower revenue sharing block grant; and Title IV-A was replaced by the Title XX social services block grant (Hill, 1981).

Since block grants have little federal oversight and do not distribute funds on the basis of economic need, many suburban areas with low levels of unemployment, substandard housing, and poverty received sizable CETA, CDBG, and Title XX funds. Several high-level evaluations revealed that minorities and other economically disadvantaged groups benefitted less from the decentralized block grants of the 1970s than they had from many of the centralized categorical programs of the 1960s. During the Carter administration, attempts were made to retarget the Nixon block grants to low-income groups and communities (Hill et al. 1993).

The Reagan administration further diluted targeting to the poor by creating more block grant programs: including Community Services, Maternal and Child Health, Preventive Health and Health Services, Alcohol, Drug Abuse and Mental Health, Low-Income Energy Assistance, and Social Services (which absorbed Title XX).

Although Nixon's CETA block grant was replaced in 1982 by another block grant--the Job Training and Partnership Act (JTPA) --The CDBG remained unchanged. Congress, as well as state governments, successfully opposed the Reagan administration's efforts to transform AFDC into a block grant. In exchange for giving the states greater flexibility in determining the target population of the block grants, funding levels for programs consolidated into block grants were reduced by 20 percent.

## Reagan Budget Cuts

Black families (and most low-income Americans) were also acutely affected by the deep budget cuts of the Reagan Administration during the 1980s. The administration disproportionately reduced spending for programs targeted to low-income people. By fiscal 1985, annual AFDC funding was cut by $1.4 billion; food stamps by $42 billion; low-income energy assistance by $0.2 billion; child nutrition by $1.4 billion; and Medicaid by $0.7 billion.

Most of the cuts in programs for the poor were achieved by tightening eligibility requirements for the working poor and reducing the value of cash and noncash benefits. The Omnibus Budget Reduction Act (OBRA) cuts in 1981 removed between four to five hundred thousand working poor families from the welfare rolls, and eliminated about one million persons from the food stamps programs. At the same time, about three hundred thousand working poor families that remained on AFDC experienced sharp reductions in cash and in-kind benefits because of increased work disincentives. Evaluations of those budget cuts revealed that increased economic hardship was experienced by thousands of poor children and their families--black and white (Palmer and Sawhill 1984).

## Tax Reform Act

The 1986 Tax Reform Act expanded the Earned Income Tax Credit (EITC) for poor working families. EITC was enacted to reduce the excessive burden of payroll taxes on the poor because many of them were paying higher effective rates than rich individuals or corporations. EITC provides a rebate to working poor families, even if their income is so low that they do not have to pay income taxes. The Tax Reform Act of 1986 not only exempted thousands of working poor families from paying taxes but also raised the thresholds of the personal exemption, standard deduction, and the EITC. In addition, these thresholds were indexed, for the first time, to keep them even with rising inflation. About three million working poor families (one-fourth of whom were black) with children were removed from the income tax rolls due to this legislation.

## Family Support Act

In addition to the expansion of EITC, Congress passed several other pro-family acts during the Reagan administration. One was the Family Support Act of 1988 that was reached by a consensus of Democrats and Republicans. While this Act mandated that welfare recipients participate in job training programs, it also insured that state welfare agencies would meet their responsibilities.

Some of the key provisions of the Family Support Act include: (1) Job Opportunities and Basic Skills Training (JOBS), a comprehensive education, training and employment program, replaced the ineffective Work Incentive (WIN) program; (2) states must guarantee child care for welfare mothers who are required to participate in JOBS; (3) child care and Medicaid coverage must be extended for twelve months for the families of recipients who leave welfare rolls due to employment; and (4) there is a mandated extension of the AFDC-Unemployed Parent (AFDC-UP) program to all fifty states.

The 1988 Family Support Act, however, has a number of deficiencies: (1) It does not mandate increases in the AFDC benefit levels. (2) It does not set nationwide minimum AFDC needs and payment standards. (3) It allows newly-participating states the option of limiting participation in the AFDC-UP program to six months. (4) It fails to assign high priority to enhancing the employability of low-income and young noncustodial fathers. However, as a result of the severe 1990-91 recession, few states could provide adequate matching to effectively implement the Family Support Act.

## Welfare Block Grant

During his 1994 presidential campaign, Bill Clinton pledged to "end welfare as we know it." Clearly, the Republican-led Congress tried to help the president to fulfill this promise by transforming and decentralizing federal welfare programs into a block grant to be administered by state governments. After vetoing two prior Republican welfare reform proposals, President Clinton signed the Personal Responsibility and Work Opportunity Reconciliation Act of 1996 (P.L. 104-193) in August 1996. This act, which went into effect 1 October 1996, has nine titles. Title 1, "Block Grants for Temporary Assistance for Needy Families" (TANF) establishes a welfare block grant that eliminates the federal open-ended entitlement of cash assistance to poor children and families. TANF repeals Aid to Families with Dependent Children (AFDC), Job Opportunities and Basic Skills (JOBS) and Emergency Assistance (EA) programs.

This legislation gives states a block grant, with a fixed amount of money, to run their programs for needy families. States must meet minimum work participation rates from 25 percent of the welfare caseload in fiscal year 1997 to 50 percent or more by 2002 and beyond. TANF also sets time limits: All recipients must have a job within two years, or they will be terminated from assistance; and they cannot receive cash assistance for total spells of recipiency of more than five years. Child care is provided for TANF recipients who find work through a Child Care and Development Block Grant (CCDBG). It also permits states to: (a) set a family cap to deny benefits to recipients who have children while on welfare; (b) limit or deny cash aid to teenage parents; and (c) require that unwed teen parents are in school and living in home with an adult.

Although the welfare block grant might succeed in reducing the welfare rolls, we do not think it will be successful in lifting from poverty most families who leave the rolls. The employment that most TANF recipients will obtain are likely to be low-wage jobs for relatively short periods of time, without any health benefits. Since states will not have sufficient funds to provide child care and medical benefits to recipients in such jobs for extended periods of time, the TANF recipients will not be able to remain employed. More importantly, this legislation is likely to lead to record-level increases in the homeless population and in the foster care placement of children whose families are terminated from TANF.

## News Media Coverage

When it comes to the treatment of black families, most coverage by the print, broadcast and TV media is unbalanced. They focus mainly on a small fraction of unrepresentative "dysfunctional" black families. Perennial attention is given to black families on welfare despite the fact that they account for only one-fifth of all black families. Equal coverage is not given to poor white families who outnumber blacks on welfare. These stories usually focus on the most deprived or exotic among the black poor for sensationalism or to win Pulitzer prizes for journalism. It should be remembered that former *Washington Post* reporter Janet Cooke was awarded a Pulitzer Prize in April 1981 for her story about an eight-year old black child Jimmy who was injected with heroin by his parents. Yet this prize was rescinded after it was revealed that the reporter had fabricated the entire story.

Coverage of black women invariably focus on their out-of-wedlock children, their dependence on welfare, or their drug addiction. Working-class black women who are in the work force, who manage to get off welfare, who have only in-wedlock children, and are not drug abusers are rarely covered in similar detail. At the same time, coverage of black men tend to focus on them as drug sellers, pimps, gang members, criminals, school dropouts, or "deadbeat dads" who provide no support for their children. It is not that there should be no coverage of such men, since they exist, but the larger numbers of black men who do not use or sell drugs, are not members of gangs, who graduate from high school, and who support their children are rarely given similar coverage.

The media also employ double standards in their news coverage of the white and black poor. First of all, stories on the white poor rarely, if ever, refer to a "white underclass," while stories on the black poor contain excessive references to a "black underclass." Second, stories on the white poor focus on external causes (recessions, technology changes, plant closings, etc.), while stories on the black poor omit references to external causes, and focus mainly on behavioral factors (such as "underclass values," low work ethics, or being reared in a female-headed family). Third, stories on the white poor usually end on a note of hope or optimism, while stories on the black poor invariably end with hopelessness or pessimism. And, fourth, stories on the white poor identify both problems and solutions, while most stories on the black poor focus almost solely on identifying problems.

It should be noted that content analyses of the media reveal that they often contain more positive stories than they are given credit. However, the positive stories are not given the prominence or the space that is devoted to the negative stories (Berry and Mitchell-Kernan 1982; Jackson 1982).

## SOLUTION IDENTIFICATION

Finally, the solutions framework must involve identification of factors at the societal, community, family, and individual levels that enhance the ability of African American families to overcome and resolve the major problems and challenges that confront them. At the center of such an assessment should be the identification of cultural strengths and effective coping strategies in the African American community that enhance black family functioning. Moreover, such a framework should involve identifying societal policies and programs that are likely to have the strongest effects on strengthening African American families.

Phillip Bowman's (1995) paradigm of four conceptual models for conducting research on the black community facilitates the identification of resiliency factors at the family and society levels. According to Bowman's typology, research studies of the black poor vary along two dimensions: (a) an emphasis on maladaptive or adaptative behavioral patterns, and (b) an emphasis on internal or external causal factors. Correlating these dimensions yields four types of studies: (1) social pathology, which explain maladaptive behavior based on internal deficits (such as underclass values, welfare dependency); (2) postindustrial dislocation, which explain maladaptive behavior based on external factors (such as racism, deindustrialization, spatial mismatch); (3) ethnic resource, which explain adaptive behavior based on indigenous cultural strengths (such as kinship bonds, religious orientation, flexible family roles); and (4) mainstream coping, which explain adaptative behavior based on external factors (employment and educational opportunities, affirmative action, pro-family policies, etc.). This volume will concentrate on Bowman's types three (ethnic resource) and four (mainstream coping) in order to identify factors internal and external to African American families that enhance their social and economic functioning and resiliency **(table 3)**.

## Family Strengths

Several solution-oriented questions that we will attempt to address are: (a) What are black family strengths? (b) How do studies of resilience mechanisms enhance our knowledge about family strengths? (c) What is known about public policies and community-based strategies that appear to be successful in strengthening black and low-income families?

Before we discuss our definition of family strengths, it is important to specify our definition of the family. We think it is essential to incorporate the African concept of family into our definition of the African American family. Operationally, we define black families as networks of households related by blood, marriage, or function that provide basic instrumental and expressive functions of the family to the members of those networks. Such family networks also include "fictive kin," that is, unrelated persons who perform important family functions. In short, we define the African American family as equivalent to the "extended family," that is, networks of functionally-related individuals who reside in *different* households. However, to retain comparability with Census Bureau classifications, we characterize related individuals who reside in the *same* households as an "immediate family," regardless of the number of generations residing there.

What are family strengths? Because of the subjectivity of the concept, it is not easy to specify what is meant by a "family strength." A strength, according to one set of criteria, could easily be interpreted as a weakness, according to another set of criteria, and vice versa. For example, most observers would probably agree that a strong bond of affection between members of a family is usually an asset, but if this affection is manifested in incestuous

**Table 3:   BOWMAN'S TYPOLOGY OF RESEARCH MODELS**

*BEHAVIORAL PATTERNS*

| *Causal Factors* | *Maladaptive* | *Adaptive* |
|---|---|---|
| Internal | Social Pathology | Ethnic Resource |
| External | Postindustrial Dislocation | Mainstream Coping |

*Source*: Bowman (1995)

relationships among family members, such a bond would generally be characterized as a liability.

We also consider family strengths to be cultural assets that are transmitted through socialization from generation to generation and are not merely adaptations or coping responses to contemporary racial or economic oppression (McDaniel 1994). We strongly concur with the conclusions reached by anthropologist Joyce Aschenbrenner (1975):

Some writers have been cognizant of strong ties among Black kindred; they have focused on the makeup of households and on kinship networks as adaptive strategies, using concepts such as "matrilocality" and "personal kindred" to characterize them. The Black family is viewed by these writers as essentially an adjustment to urban ghetto conditions, rather than as a continuing institution. The emphasis on household organization and on adaptation results in overlooking important aspects of family ties through space and time by means of conscious and ritualized practices in funerals, reunions, and regular visiting patterns. . . .A comparison of my conclusions with those of studies of Southern and Caribbean families reveals similarities that support the view of the Black family as a

cultural institution with a long tradition, rather than an adaptation
to specific conditions. (Aschenbrenner 1975, 6)

Diana Slaughter and Gerald McWorter (1985) also emphasize the
cultural continuity of black family strengths:

> If the black extended family is an American adaptation of a
> longstanding African tradition, then clear cultural links to the
> diaspora is implied and can be expected to continue. This would
> occur because of a people's thrust for cultural continuity, even in a
> changed geographical setting (i.e, urban by comparison to rural). If
> it is merely a self-help or survival unit, then the black extended
> family will wane in scope and influence in accordance with any
> societal change which heralds significant social and economic
> improvements for black people. (Slaughter and McWorter 1985, 16)

Operationally, we define as family strengths those traits that
facilitate the ability of the family to meet the needs of its members
and the demands made upon it by systems outside the family unit.
They are necessary for the survival, maintenance, and advancement
of family networks. Moreover, a family's strength is not determined
by its ability to function in only one area but in various domains of
the family. For example, Ludwig Geismar's (1973) pioneering scale
of family functioning identifies eight domains: family relationships
and unity; individual behavior and adjustment; care and training
of children; social activities; economic practices; home and
household resources; health conditions and practices; and use of
community resources. His longitudinal study of black and Hispanic
adolescent single mothers found that these families were "strong"
in some domains and "weak" in others. Moreover, the importance
of different domains varied depending on the stage of their life
cycles. Thus, we assume that our five family strengths will, on
average, have positive or functional consequences for most of the
domains of black family functioning.

Based on the works of W. E. B. Du Bois (1909), Franklin Frazier (1939), Hylan Lewis (1967), and Andrew Billingsley (1968), we identified in our 1972 work the following five attributes as functional for the survival, stability, and advancement of black families: strong achievement orientation, strong work orientation, flexible family roles, strong kinship bonds, and strong religious orientation. Although these traits can be found among other racial and ethnic groups, we contend that these strengths have operated differently among blacks because of their unique history of slavery and other racial oppression. Thus, in this twenty-five year update, we will focus on the same five family strengths.

However, we think it is important to note that several studies of black families have identified similar and other strengths (Giovannoni and Billingsley 1970; Ladner 1974; Stack 1974; Woodson 1981; Hall and King 1982; Williams 1987; Sandven and Resnick 1990; Williams and Kornblum 1994; Jarrett 1995). In a pioneering study of cultural adaptations among blacks, Hispanics, Asians, and American Indians, Algae Harrison and others (1990) identified the following as cultural assets of people of color: extendedness, role flexibility, biculturalism, collectivism, and spirituality. Moreover, an in-depth study of strong black families was conducted by Howard University Institute for Urban Affairs and Research (Gary et al. 1983). A major goal of this study was to identify the correlates of strong black families. The study's sample comprised fifty black families who were nominated as "strong" in the Washington, D.C. area. Half were married couples and the remaining were female-headed.

The two attributes that were most often cited by the respondents, regardless of family structure, as common strengths were family unity and religious orientation. Other strengths mentioned were: love, effective coping strategies, mutual support, and sharing responsibilities. A survey of blacks conducted by David Royce and Gladys Turner (1980) identified the following family strengths:

teaching children to respect themselves, teaching children how to be happy, stressing cooperation in the family, and disciplining children. Janice Hale-Benson (1982) also identifies several other black family strengths related to the socialization of black children.

**Resilience Mechanisms**

Research on resilience by psychiatrists, psychologists, pediatricians, and sociologists have advanced markedly our understanding of the complex processes that facilitate the development of stress-resistent children. Many of these studies have involved longitudinal studies of the development of children of disadvantaged or mentally or physically handicapped parents in order to identify the risk factors that increase their vulnerability for negative outcomes and the protective factors that enhance their resilience for positive outcomes.

We think that Michael Rutter's (1967) research on resilience mechanisms provides a useful theoretical framework for understanding family strengths. Rutter characterizes resilience not as a fixed attribute of the individual but as a protective mechanism that affects the individual's response to a risk or stressful situation and operates at critical turning points during various stages of one's life cycle. Therefore, he does not refer to resilience factors but to resilience mechanisms and processes.

Linda Winfield (1991) underscores the following issues in conducting research on resilience in the field of education:

> Rather, the critical issue for policy and instruction center around identifying the protective processes and mechanisms that reduce risk and foster resilience. How do protective processes operate at different developmental levels or transition points in the schooling process? Are the variables and functions the same for different race, ethnic, and gender groups? More important, what can schools,

administrators, teachers, community groups, and policymakers do to enhance and foster the development of these (protective) processes? (Winfield 1991, 7)

Rutter describes four protective mechanisms that are likely to enhance resilience: (1) the reduction of negative outcomes by altering either the risk or the child's exposure to the risk; (2) the reduction of a negative chain reaction following risk exposure; (3) the establishment and maintenance of self-esteem and self-efficacy; and (4) the opening up of opportunities.

We find most of Rutter's protective processes to contribute to the enhancement of various black family strengths, such as achievement orientation (which includes self-esteem and locus of control), and reinforcing a strong work orientation by eliminating racial barriers to employment opportunities. Several important studies on resilience mechanisms among black youths have been conducted by a number of scholars (Winfield 1991; Nettles and Pleck 1994). More research on the relationship of resilience mechanisms to the operation of various family strengths of different racial and ethnic groups is urgently needed (McAdoo 1991; Denby 1996).

Yet, it has been ethnographic studies that have increased our understanding markedly of various *processes* in black families that enhance the resilience of low-income black children and youth. (Lewis 1967; Stack 1974; Clark 1983; Malson 1986; Burton 1995) In a unique and insightful review of ethnographic studies of African American families, Robin Jarrett (1995) sought to identify family processes that facilitated upward mobility of low-income black youth.

Based on a careful analysis of the content of twenty-seven studies, Jarrett identified the following five "community-bridging" patterns that serve as a bridge between the family and positive support systems in the community:

(1)  *Supportive Adult Network Structure.*  Families that rely on kinship networks, including fictive kin, to assist in the rearing and support of their children.

(2)  *Restricted Family-Community Relations.*  Families that try to prevent or minimize their children's contact with "bad or undesirable" individuals, groups, or neighborhoods.

(3)  *Stringent Parental Monitoring Strategies.*  Families that carefully monitor and supervise the time, space, and friendships of adolescents through a wide range of strategies, including interviewing peers, curfews, chaperons, etc.

(4)  *Strategic Alliances with Mobility-Enhancing Institutions and Organizations.*  Families that seek to have their children participate in mobility-enhancing institutions, such as church, Sunday School, Scouts, public school, parochial school, etc.

(5)  *Adult-Sponsored Youth Development.*  Families that try to enhance the competence and skills of their children by encouraging them to assume various responsibilities, including part-time work, household chores, caring for younger siblings, etc.

According to Jarrett, these five characteristics represent active strategies that many socially mobile low-income parents use to mediate or counteract the negative influences of their current environment on their children. She also recommends that youth-serving organizations should design their outreach programs for low-income black families to complement and reinforce these coping patterns by parents. More qualitative and quantitative studies are needed that examine the effectiveness of the five patterns and other mobility strategies by parents in low-income black families.

# Chapter 2

# THE AFRICAN HERITAGE

Our study will adopt the historical perspective used in the first in-depth study of black families *The Negro American Family*, by W. E. B. Du Bois, which was published in 1909. In this pioneering work, Du Bois made it clear that black family life could not be properly understood without first examining family patterns in Africa:

> In each case an attempt has been made to connect present conditions with the African past. This is not because Negro Americans are Africans, or can trace an unbroken social history from Africa, but because there is a distinct nexus between Africa and America which, though broken and perverted, is nevertheless not to be neglected by the careful student. (Du Bois 1909, 9)

Melville Herskovits (1938-39) also underscores the importance of examining the degree of influence of the African cultural heritage by scientists who study race relations or black family life:

> When we are confronted with psychological studies of race relations made in utter ignorance of characteristic African patterns of motivation and behavior, or with sociological analyses of Negro family life which make not the slightest attempt to take into account even the chance that the phenomena being studied might in some way have been influenced by the carry-over of certain African traditions . . . .we can but wonder about the value of such work. (Herskovits 1938-39, 93)

Niara Sudarkasa (1980) emphasizes the cultural unity of the African heritage:

> . . . most of the Africans enslaved in America came from continguous areas in the western part of the continent where there had been a long history of culture contact and a high degree of institutional similarity. . . .
>
> Thus, regardless of the "diverse" backgrounds of the Africans enslaved in America (a diversity that is usually greatly exaggerated), there was a commonality in the familial patterns known to them. It was this shared social organizational "baseline" that enabled the Africans enslaved in

America to create recognizably African patterns where they lived. . . .If Israelites enslaved in Egypt for centuries could remain Israelites; if diverse European peoples in the twentieth century can still acknowledge cultural survivals from ancient Greece and Rome, I wonder why it is considered so preposterous that Africans only a few generations removed from their homelands would show evidence of their culture roots.
(Sudarkasa 1980, 52-53)

## CONJUGALITY VS. CONSANGUINITY

A major difference between family organization in Europe and Africa is their different emphasis on kinship patterns based on conjugality, marriage ties, or consanguinity, blood ties. In Europe, the conjugal unit (or the "nuclear family") is the primary building block of European family organization for household formation, decision making, property transmission, and socialization of children. On the other hand, consanguineal cores are the building blocks of African families. These consanguineal networks may include various conjugal households that contain husbands and wives or parents and children. As Sudarkasa observes:

This co-resident extended family occupied a group of adjoining or contiguous dwellings known as a compound. Upon marriage, Africans did not normally form new isolated households, but joined a compound in which the extended family of the groom, or that of the bride, was already domiciled. (Sudarkasa 1988, 31)

The stability of the African extended family does not depend on the stability of the conjugal units. Although traditional African marriages were stable, marital dissolution or divorce did not have the same effects as in nuclear family systems. When divorces did occur, they were usually followed by remarriage. The children of a divorced couple were usually brought up in their original compound (or by members of their lineage residing elsewhere), even though the divorcing parent had left that compound. In short, instability of conjugal units through divorce or death did not often have detrimental consequences for their members because of the stability of extended family networks. In traditional African societies, spouses could come and go, but the (extended) family would remain intact (Foster 1983). According to Sudarkasa (1988):

Once a marriage took place, if the demands of the conjugal relationship came into irreconcilable conflict with consanguineal commitments, the former would often be sacrificed. Instead of interpreting instances of marital instability as prima facie evidence of family instability, it should be realized that the fragility of the conjugal relationship could be a consequence or corollary of the stability of the consanguineal family network. Historically, such groups survived by nurturing a strong sense of responsibility among members and by fostering a code of reciprocity which could strain relations with persons not bound by it. (Sudarkasa 1988, 40)

Joyce Aschenbrenner (1975) also underscores the priority of blood ties over marital ties in her study of black families in Chicago:

Discussions of the breakdown of the Black family have usually focused on the marital relationship. This emphasis reflects the overriding importance of the marriage tie in our society, rather than any peculiarity of the Black family. In societies with extended families, other relationships, such as father-son, mother-daughter, or brother-sister, may be more important in terms of social and economic support than that of husband and wife. . . . Among Black people in the United States. . . . the marital tie does not enjoy the central and absolute status it generally holds among middle-class Whites, who create a socially and economically independent family unit. (Aschenbrenner 1975, 3)

It is also important to point out that African conjugal units are not *nuclear families* in the common usage of the term. They are actual or potential polygamous families (usually involving polygyny, a plurality of wives). The normal development of a conjugal unit would involve a monogamous and then a polygamous phase. The custom of marrying the widow of one's deceased brother was one element of traditional polygyny. However, whether a man had one wife or many wives and children, it was considered *one* family. As Sudarkasa observes:

Although Africans recognize the mother-child dyad as a primary social and affective unit, . . . . it is erroneous to characterize this unit as a separate "nuclear family" within the African extended family. Such a formulation has no explanatory value since none of the normal functions of a family [was] traditionally performed by this unit in isolation. It was not a unit of socialization in and of itself; it was not a unit of economic production or consumption in and of itself; it was not an isolated unit of emotional

support or mutual aid; it obviously was not a procreative unit. Why then
term it a "nuclear family"?  (Sudarkasa 1980, 44)

More importantly, even the husband-wife-children triad in Africa should
not be characterized as a *nuclear family*, since this unit does not provide
socialization, economic production, or emotional support by itself in
isolation. In short, the conjugal units in Africa do not perform all of the
traditional functions of a family, because those functions are performed by
the extended family networks. Thus, the African extended family is *the*
African family, while the conjugal or "nuclear" family is *the* European
family.

It should be pointed out that African extended families also comprise
"para-kin," or "fictive kin," that is, members who are not related by blood
or marriage. Since these nonrelated individuals perform important functions
of the family, such as socialization of children, economic production, and
emotional support, they are considered to be members of such extended
families. Thus, many unrelated African extended family members are
considered to be surrogate fathers, mothers, grandmothers, grandfathers,
aunts, uncles, brothers, sisters, and cousins because of the important family
functions they perform.

However, as Sudarkasa (1988) notes, it should be clearly stated that the
isolated family headed by a formerly married or never married woman with
children is *not* part of the African cultural legacy.  Such households were
either part of a larger network of extended family members or were taken
into the households of male relatives.

## MALE AND FEMALE ROLES

While the European family is only patrilineal, that is, characterized by
descent through the male line, African families are most often patrilineal but
may also be matrilineal, that is, characterized by descent through the female
line. In African family lineage, a kin group are relations, both living and
deceased, who trace their descent from a common ancestor through a
mother or father, but not through both. In the case of a patrilineal society,
a woman's children, male and female, belong to the lineage to which their
respective fathers belong but *not* to their mother's lineage.  A woman's
children would belong to a lineage comprising their father and his sisters
and brothers sired by the same father; their father's father and his sisters
and brothers of the same father, and so on.

However, in a matrilineal society, a woman's children, male and female, belong to the lineage to which she belongs. That lineage would also include her brothers and sisters born of the same mother; her mother and her mother's brothers and sisters born of the same mother; her mother's mother, and so on.

Although lineages are based only on descent, extended families are based on descent *and* marriage. In the lineage, descent is traced unilaterally, through one line only, but in the extended family, filiation is traced bilaterally, through both parents. Thus, in a patrilineal or matrilineal society, the lineage is composed of relatives linked through the father-line or the mother-line. In both types of society, the extended family comprises relatives on both the mother's and the father's side. Lineages are considered as existing in perpetuity, involving the living and dead, going back to the founding ancestor. Extended families, on the other hand, are networks of living relatives.

If the wife joined the extended family of the groom, the household was patrilocal. However, if the husband joined the extended family of the wife, the household was matrilocal. Only one of the spouses changed residence at marriage because the other was already living in the compound of the extended family.

Because women tend to have higher status in African families than they do in European families, the African family system has been characterized incorrectly as *matriarchal*. Women have high status in African extended families in both patrilineal and matrilineal societies. Women married into the compound give the patrilineage continuity, which has a significance that transcends their relationship to the men who happen to be their husbands. As wives and mothers, the women of a lineage form the connecting links with other lineages. Thus they are important to their husband's kin as well as to their husbands. Because of the important role of women, divorce was rare in most African societies.

The attachment between a mother and her children tends to be closer than those between a father and his children. This means that the responsibilities for rearing, feeding, and supervising are much more the province of the mother than the father. However, in addition to their domestic and homemaking responsibilities, African mothers also play important roles as economic providers. As Herskovits (1941) observes:

> The open-air market is the effective agent in the retail distributive process, and business, as in West Africa, is principally in the hands of women. It is

customary for them to handle the family resources, and their economic independence as traders makes for their personal independence, something which, within the family, gives them power such as is denied to women who, in accordance with the prevalent European custom, are dependent upon their husbands for support. In both West Africa and the West Indies the women, holding their economic destinies in their own hands, are fully capable of going their ways if their husbands displease them; not being hampered by any conception of marriage as an ultimate commitment, separation is easily effected and a consequent fluidity in family personnel. . . . (Herskovits 1941, 180-81)

However, Herskovits (1941) warns against inferring that the important role of women in African society means men have a subordinate status:

Yet it must not be forgotten that the economic and social role of the man in Negro society is of the utmost significance in rounding out the picture of Negro social life. . . .Despite the place of women in the West African family, the unit holds a prominent place for the husband and father who, as head of the polygynous group, is the final authority over its members, sharing fully in all those obligations which the family must meet if it is to survive and hold its place in the stable society of which it forms a part. (Herskovits 1941, 175-76)

African families exhibit great flexibility of roles and egalitarian patterns between men and women. Besides engaging in economic activities, such as farming, hunting, fishing, etc, men also perform important domestic functions, such as the socialization and disciplining of children, and assisting in performing other household duties, including meal preparation. M. Fortes (1967), for example, describes marital relations among the Ashanti as follows:

The result, in practice, is that there is a high degree of equality between the sexes. In terms of personal behavior and attitudes, there is often no apparent difference between the relations of mother and children and those of father and children. (Fortes 1967, 269-70)

While European societies socialize children into rigid or "dual" conceptions of "masculinity" and "femininity," African societies exhibit much flexibility and overlap in the sex role expectations of males and females. As Diane Lewis (1975) observes:

Behavior which is associated with the male role in Euro-American culture is associated with both males and females in this (black) community. . . .Both husband and wife have authority in the home; both are responsible for the economic support of the family; both take the initiative in forming and breaking up a marriage and both may find separation to their advantage.

Not only is behavior considered appropriate for males in white culture displayed by both women and men in black culture, but behavior which is associated with females in white culture is characteristic of both men and women in black culture. (Lewis 1975, 229-30)

## IMPORTANCE OF CHILDREN

African societies tend to be child-centered. They place high value on children. Nobles (1974, 15) observes that this importance is "deeply rooted in our African heritage and philosophical orientation which. . . .places a special value on children because they represent the continuity of life." Fortes (1967) observes:

The Ashanti regard the bond between mother and child as the keystone of all social relations. Childlessness is felt by both men and women as the greatest of all personal tragedies and humiliations. Prolific child-bearing is honored. A mother of ten boasts of her achievement and is given a ceremony of congratulations. (Fortes 1967, 262)

Moreover, M. Kenyatta (1983) asserts:

I hold very strongly that black families are neither patriarchal nor matriarchal nor even matrifocal per se. Rather, the black family is best understood as child-centered, as oriented toward reproduction and sustenance of black life in the context of a racist society, mindful of the genocidal potential of the dominant culture. (Kenyatta 1983, 20-21)

James King (1976) also observes this emphasis on children:

If one considers that every child in the black community belongs to the entire black community, then it will be easier to grasp the importance Black Americans give to black children. How often has one heard that black women have too many illegitimate babies? How often has one heard that black women should be forced to practice birth control? What such questions overlook is the fact that in the black community there is no such thing as an illegitimate child. The children are loved and cared for by the entire community. (King 1976, 157)

The greater reluctance of black women to have abortions compared with white women has been attributed to a cultural legacy that values children highly--whether born in-wedlock or out-of-wedlock. Moreover, the cultural primacy of black children is also reflected in the fact that black babies born out-of-wedlock are more likely to be kept within the immediate or extended family, while white out-of-wedlock babies are more likely to be placed with formal adoption agencies.

## INFORMAL ADOPTION

Many social scientists have examined the informal practices of child rearing in the black community (Stack 1974; Furtstenberg 1981; Sandven and Resnick 1990). Andrew Miller (1993) identified the pervasiveness of informal adoption or "child fosterage" among blacks in Africa, the Caribbean and the United States. His analyses affirm the cross-cultural unity of this practice among black extended families:

> Studies of extended, multihousehold African American families over the last twenty years have all hinted at African origins for these practices but have not been able to build historical links. They also have not emphasized the role of child fosterage in these families, though all of their work includes clear and prominent evidence of child fosterage among African Americans in both rural and urban areas. . . .Whether the African heritage in America manifests itself in survivals, reinterpretations, syncretisms, or any type of combination thereof, it is still present as a history and an influence. . . .That fosterage remains a significant family choice in contemporary Africa as well as in the United States, however, even with Africa's extremely different social structures, points to reasons for fosterage that transcend the coping strategies or survival tactics of African Americans. The reasons lie in its African heritage. (Miller 1993, 280)

## BICULTURAL SOCIALIZATION

Many scholars (Dixon and Foster 1971; Valentine 1971; Lewis 1975; Hale-Benson 1982; Pinderhughes 1982; Boykin and Toms 1985) contend that African cultural residuals are transmitted from generation to generation by black Americans through bicultural socialization. Such patterns of dual socialization facilitate the acculturation of blacks to mainstream and African American cultural patterns simultaneously. Du Bois (1903) highlighted this duality in the following classic statement:

> . . .the Negro is a sort of seventh son, born with a veil, and gifted with second-sight in this American world--a world which yields him no true self-consciousness, but only lets him see himself through the revelation of the other world. It is a peculiar sensation, this double consciousness. . . .One ever feels his twoness--an American, a Negro; two souls, two thoughts, two unreconciled strivings; two warring ideals in one dark body, whose dogged strength alone keeps it from being torn asunder. (Du Bois 1903, 45)

According to many scholars (Valentine 1971; Lewis 1975; Baratz and Baratz 1970), biculturation helps to explain the consistency of differences between blacks and whites regarding family organization, fertility patterns, child rearing, learning styles, linguistic patterns, religious behavior, funeral rituals, nutrition, and song, and dance. However, as Wade Boykin and Forrest Toms (1985) note, African continuities are often transmitted unconsciously by black Americans as traditional or habitual values, beliefs, behaviors, and customs:

> Of course, we cannot rule out that black cultural values or beliefs are overtly taught per se. But if and when it happens, it typically is done without awareness that they are embedded within a comprehensive cultural complex of West African origin. . . .This, then, is a tacit socialization process. Tacit because, for all intents and purposes, black parents typically are unaware that they are transmitting cultural styles or even cultural values. (Boykin and Toms 1985, 42)

Yet, not all black families have the same ability to provide bicultural socialization. Elaine Pinderhughes (1982) observes:

> Some Afro-American families are comfortable with biculturality; they are unusually strong, flexible, tolerant of ambiguity, and creative in dealing with the American and victim systems. Other Afro-American families are not comfortable with biculturality; for them, dealing with the two different value systems creates a conflict in values and a confusion about identity. (Pinderhughes 1982, 94)

Increasingly, research studies (Dixon and Foster 1971; Hale-Benson 1982) demonstrate that bicultural socialization is facilitated among blacks because of the African cultural capacity to synthesize opposites or polarities. Lewis (1975) explains this process as follows:

> The Afro-American cultural orientation, the bringing together of polarities, stands in direct contrast to the Euro-American concern with dualities. Mainstream culture is understood in the setting up of linguistic, analytic, and moral dichotomies, such as subject/object; mind/body; good/bad; sacred/profane, etc. Afro-American culture, however, is characterized by unity and synthesis. Lerone Bennett (1964) notes that the black tradition affirms that good and bad, creative and destructive, wise and foolish, up and down, are inseparable facets of existence. Therefore these polarities are not conceptualized as dichotomies. He finds that the existential unit expressed in "good is bad," is in conflict with the Euro-American dichotomy, "either good or bad."   (Lewis 1975, 225-26)

## CARIBBEAN BLACKS

We cannot end this discussion about the African influence on black Americans without also acknowledging the Caribbean influence. Many Americans fail to realize that millions of enslaved Africans who were brought to this country came from the Caribbean and not directly from Africa. In fact, the overwhelming majority of African slaves were brought to the West Indies and South America, and not to North America. That is why, even today, the largest number of blacks who reside outside of Africa live in Brazil.

Blacks of Caribbean origin continue to make important contributions to the advancement of black Americans. Yet, it is ironic, that there are relatively few in-depth research studies that focus on Caribbean blacks in America. The classic study *The Negro Immigrant* by eminent black sociologist Ira DeA. Reid (1939) has not been matched by any scholar in over fifty years. However, many black scholars (Bryce-LaPorte 1973; Palmer 1974; Bryce-LaPorte and Mortimer 1973; Bryce-LaPorte 1980; Millette 1990)--most of them of Caribbean origin--have enhanced markedly our understanding of Caribbean blacks in America.

Most references to West Indian blacks in the research literature are just those --references. Typically, the "high" achievement of West Indians is usually touted by some scholars (Sowell 1978; Glazer and Moynihan, 1963) as proof of the insignificance of racism as a major reason for the "low" achievement of black Americans. These analysts assert that the superior socialization of children in Caribbean families accounts for the higher achievement of West Indians relative to native blacks.

Based on his analysis of 1970 census data relating to West Indian blacks in New York, Thomas Sowell (1978) found that their incomes were not only much higher than those of native blacks but almost as high as whites. He also found that West Indian blacks had higher levels of educational attainment, family stability and labor force participation than native blacks. Thus, he concludes that the high priority that West Indians placed on achievement was responsible for their higher accomplishments. Yet Sowell never bothered to explain why the academic performance and income levels of West Indian blacks in England were so much lower than those of whites.

Interestingly, analyses of the 1980 census data by Reynolds Farley and Walter Allen (1987) strongly refute the findings of Sowell. These researchers found family income, family stability, and labor force patterns to be comparable between foreign-born and native-born blacks. Only in the area of educational attainment were native-born blacks at a disadvantage to foreign-born blacks. Farley and Allen (1978, 405) conclude, "Most claims concerning the achievement of West Indian blacks in the United States are greatly exaggerated."

A comparative analysis by Robert Hill (1983) of Caribbean blacks and native blacks based on the NUL Black Pulse Survey, a nationally representative survey of 3,000 black households conducted in 1979-80, revealed findings similar to those of Farley and Allen. In order to obtain more accurate national-level data on Caribbean blacks, the National Urban League's Research Department placed an ethnic origins question directed to Caribbeans in its Black Pulse Survey in the fall and winter of 1979-80. The question was: "Are you of West Indian or other Caribbean descent?" The Black Pulse Survey obtained the same proportion (3 percent) of foreign-born blacks as did the 1980 census, but, more importantly, it revealed that 10 percent of the blacks in the United States--not 2 or 3 percent--were of Caribbean descent. Hill estimated that the Caribbean black population in the United States in 1980 was about 2.5 million--more than three times larger than their numbers in the 1980 census, and three-fourths of these Caribbean blacks lived in the state of New York.

Hill's analysis (Billingsley 1992) reveals that Caribbean blacks had more in common with native blacks than differences. Thirty-three percent of Caribbean blacks were in higher-paying professional and craft jobs, compared with 31 percent of native blacks. The proportion of middle-income households (with $20,000 or more income) was about the same between Caribbean (18 percent) and native (20 percent) blacks. However, the proportion of household heads with some college education was somewhat higher among Caribbean (28 percent) than native (21 percent) blacks. On the other hand, the proportion of female-headed families was much higher among Caribbean (58 percent) than native (46 percent) blacks. A comparative analysis by Model (1995) of West Indians and African Americans in the New York metropolitan area based on the 1970, 1980, and 1990 censuses also did not find strong support for the vaunted superiority of Caribbean blacks over African Americans.

How do we explain the differences between the findings of Sowell's study and subsequent analyses? A major reason is the change in immigration laws. Prior to 1965, the racially exclusive Immigration Act of 1924 reduced markedly non-white immigrants, especially from the Caribbean and Africa. Highest preference was given to persons who planned to attend college or to hold jobs in professional or skilled fields, such as nursing. However, with passage of the 1965 amendments, ceilings for Caribbean and other nonwhite countries were raised significantly, and immigrants residing in the United States were allowed to bring family members--regardlessof their educational or occupational training or expectations--to this country. This change in the immigration laws reduced the selection of immigrants with higher education and skills. Ransford Palmer's (1974) study reveals similar changes in the attributes of West Indian immigrants between 1962 and 1972. Thus, Stephen Steinberg (1995, 140) concludes, "As I have argued elsewhere, the much touted 'success' of Asians and West Indians is largely an artifact of selective migration--that is, the influx of large numbers of professionals and other educated and skilled workers" (Steinberg, 1991).

Unfortunately, most recent references made to West Indian blacks in the media are stereotypically negative. Numerous news articles focus on "Jamaican posses" that are reputed to be responsible for most of the drug trafficking in black communities across this nation, and many motion pictures about drug dealers in inner-city areas often focus on those from Jamaica or other West Indian countries. Thus, American society has gone from one extreme to the other with respect to the portrayal of Caribbean blacks.

Clearly, the overwhelming majority of blacks of Caribbean origin have high achievement orientations, a strong work ethic, and support their families through legitimate avenues, not by selling drugs. From the days of Crispus Attucks and Prince Hall to Shirley Chisholm, Mervyn Dymally,

Colin Powell and Louis Farrakhan, blacks of Caribbean origin have deeply enriched the quality of life in the African American community by working together with native blacks on common problems and challenges. A unity of blacks of African origin throughout the Diaspora needs to be sustained, increased, and strengthened.

# Chapter 3

# Class Trends and Concept Misuse

Before we discuss recent class trends among black families, we think it is important to examine the misuse and abuse of the class concept because it often distorts our understanding of black family functioning (Lewis 1967; Herzog 1970; Lawson 1992; Steinberg 1995). Popular usage of this concept often manifests one or more of the following six errors: (a) reifying class abstractions; (b) shifting class criteria; (c) static analyses; (d) equating class with culture; (e) confusing class and race; and (f) confusing attributes with correlates.

## MISUSE OF CLASS CONCEPT

Gunnar Myrdal (1963), the Swedish economist, was one of the earliest scholars to use the term *underclass*. He used the concept to describe people who were economically marginalized by structural and labor market processes to an extent that they were unaffected by business cycles and other fluctuations in the national economy. In his classic study of the black family, Andrew Billingsley (1968, 141) also identified the "under class" as a structural concept that fell "outside and below the formal class structure." Douglas Glasgow (1981) also used a concept of the black underclass that was similar to Myrdal's emphasis on persons who were disadvantaged by structural transformations.

However, Kenneth Auletta (1982) applies a different meaning to the term *underclass*, which proved more acceptable to the general public and policy makers at the time. It was popularized in the media and was subsequently adopted by social scientists. Auletta's use of underclass shifted the core meaning of this term from the impact of societal institutions on people to the maladaptive attitudes, values, and behavior of individuals.

In his important work *The Truly Disadvantaged*, William Julius Wilson (1987) further popularized the concept of the underclass among social scientists. His research moreover stimulated numerous studies of the underclass that were funded by federal agencies and several foundations. However, his use of this term incorporated elements from both Myrdal and Auletta. Although Wilson included the long-term unemployed and poor, his inclusion of welfare recipients, school dropouts, teenage mothers, delinquents and criminals shifted most analyses and discussions of this group to the "undeserving poor," that is, persons who participate in behavior that violates societal norms. Whereas liberals used the term *underclass* to refer to class disabilities, conservatives used the term to refer to cultural disabilities. However, liberals (Lemann 1991) also incorporated cultural dimensions by equating inner-city life-styles with a culture of poverty" (or "southern heritage") patterns. In short, whether one was liberal or conservative, most analyses confounded class and culture in their assessments of the black underclass (Steinberg 1995). Moreover, both conceptions minimized the significance of contemporary racism as a major factor in creating and maintaining the underclass in the black community. Herbert Gans (1995) provides an in-depth account of the historical origins of the term as well as its significance in contemporary research and policy debates.

## REIFYING CLASS ABSTRACTIONS

One of the most frequent flaws in studies of class stratification of minorities and low-income groups is the reifying of class concepts. Reification refers to the fallacy of treating conceptual abstractions as if they existed in reality. Many commentators fail to realize that the number and composition of class categories, such as upper class, middle class, and lower class are arbitrary abstractions of reality that vary according to the objectives of the analysts. Karl Marx and Frederich Engels (1932) found it expedient to use only two class strata (the bourgeoisie and proletariat), while Lloyd Warner and Paul Lunt (1942) found it useful to employ six social classes (upper-upper, lower-upper, upper-middle, lower-middle, upper-lower and lower-lower) in their community studies. Myrdal (1944) identified the fallacy of reification in his criticism of the Warner school for treating prototypes as if they were real:

In such an approach it is of importance to keep clear at the outset that our class concepts have no other reality than as a conceptual framework. . . .We must choose our class lines arbitrarily to answer certain specific questions.

The authors of the Warner group. . . .often give the reader the impression that they believe that there are in reality clearly demarcated social classes. . . . [and] each of these classes has its distinctive patterns of familial, recreational and general social behavior. . . .

Because of this misconception. . . .which is sometimes called reification. . . .these authors become tempted to give us a somewhat over simplified idea about social stratification in the Negro community . . . .what they are actually presenting is an ideal--typical--and therefore, overtypical--description based on much detailed observation which is all organized under the conceptual scheme applied. By unduly insisting upon the realism of this analysis, however, they come to imply a rigidity in the class structure which is not really there. (Myrdal vol 2: 1944, 1130)

Wilson's analysis of the "truly disadvantaged" provides several instances of reification. He asserts, for example:

Today's ghetto neighborhoods are populated almost exclusively by the most disadvantaged segments of the black urban community, that heterogeneous grouping of families and individuals who are outside the mainstream of the American occupation system. (Wilson 1987, 8)

Although Wilson depicts ghetto neighborhoods as comprising "almost exclusively" poor and welfare families, the 1980 census data he presents for the nation's five largest central cities reveal that at least half of the residents of highly concentrated poverty areas are "working class." Within poverty areas that comprise 40 percent or more poor people, half of the families are two-parents, not poor, and not on welfare, while three out of five families have income from earnings. Consequently, half of the families in the most extreme poverty areas are, in fact, mainstream "working class" role models for the underclass. Such data sharply undermine Wilson's assertions about the "extreme isolation" of the underclass due to a paucity of individuals in the labor force in poverty neighborhoods.

In his work *Losing Ground*, Charles Murray (1984) also provides numerous examples of reification. He contends that the "poor, female-headed family on welfare" prototype is "typical" of the majority of black families living in low-income areas. Yet, data from the 1980 census reveal that poor female-headed families comprise only 25 percent of all black families in poverty areas, while poor female-headed families on welfare comprise only 16 percent of all black families living in poverty areas.

Reification is present in descriptions of the underclass in which individuals are depicted as *simultaneously* possessing certain traits: (1) in a female-headed family, (2) lacking a strong work ethic, (3) with a negative self-concept, (4) on welfare for long periods, and (5) chronically poor. Not only is this prototype representative of only a small fraction of blacks, but, more importantly, no psychological and other empirical data are provided to reveal the number of blacks who simultaneously have *all* five attributes. Such analysts fail to realize that the primary function of operational definitions, classifications, and prototypes is to abstract reality, not to mirror it. Reification of prototypes usually occurs when discussions focus on polar opposites or extremes--underclass versus middle class--and invariably omit any analyses of intermediate groups--such as working class. When analysts believe that such operational constructs reflect reality, reification impedes the development of effective strategies for understanding and combating the forces responsible for race and class inequality (Lawson 1992).

One of the few studies that attempted to obtain national data on the attitudes, values, and behavior of the "underclass" was a survey that was conducted in 1988 by Louis Harris and Associates (1989) for the NAACP Legal Defense and Educational Fund as part of a larger study of racism and poverty. This research operationally defined as underclass family households that lived in "persistently poor" (that is, 40 percent or more of the residents in poverty) census tracts *and* met at least two of the following four criteria: (1) an unemployed or underemployed adult male; (2) a high-school dropout; (3) a household member receiving AFDC; and (4) single mothers who are heads of households. Because of budgetary limitations, the survey interviewed only black households that met the "underclass" criteria and resided in one of eight major cities.

Contrary to popular belief, this survey revealed that most of the black underclass had mainstream aspirations for themselves and their children: 81 percent wanted "better job opportunities"; 80 percent wanted "more job training"; 65 percent wanted to take math or reading skills courses; 59 percent wanted their children "to stay in school"; and 55 percent wanted their children to "go to college." Thus, Harris and Associates concluded: [These]. . . .findings also contradict. . . .the widespread stereotype. . . .that the persistently poor have given up all hope of self-sufficiency and have abandoned all responsibility for their own lives."

## SHIFTING CLASS CRITERIA

One of the most frequent abuses of the class concept is the use of shifting or different criteria for denoting membership in specific class strata that are inconsistent with one's own operational definition. For example, analysts such as Wilson define the underclass as a subgroup of the poor who are characterized by *long-term* unemployment, poverty, and welfare dependency:

> Included in this group are individuals who lack training and skills and either experience long-term unemployment or are not members of the labor force, individuals who are engaged in street crime and other forms of aberrant behavior, and families that experience long-term spells of poverty and/or welfare dependency. These are the populations to which I refer when I speak of the *underclass*. (Wilson 1987, 8)

Yet, contrary to his own definition, none of the data that Wilson presents to depict the prevalence of the "underclass" in inner-city communities are based on *long-term* attributes. Instead, he employs cross-sectional data on current joblessness, poverty, and welfare dependency and fails to disaggregate the long-term from the short-term jobless, poor, and welfare recipients. By including both the short-term and long-term in his statistics, the black underclass is made to appear much larger than it actually is. Furthermore, the cross-sectional data are misconstrued as if they were, in fact, longitudinal data on poor blacks in inner cities.

Shifting class criteria have also been used in analyses of the black "middle class." At least two analysts (Wilson 1978; Landry 1988) have incorporated data on the middle class that are based on data that sometimes apply to *all* persons in white-collar jobs, at other times apply to *all* persons with a college education, and at other times apply to *all* suburban families. These different criteria weaken rather than strengthen any claim about a distinct "middle-class," since the size and composition of its members vary markedly depending on the criteria used. Moreover, these data also contain individuals and families who are working class or underclass. For example, about half of black men in sales jobs and black women in clerical occupations have poverty-level wages (Hill 1981). Such studies provide fragmented and misleading descriptions of specific socio-economic strata because of the failure to use *one* consistent set of criteria throughout the analyses.

## STATIC ANALYSES

A persistent weakness of class analyses of blacks is the absence of any vertical mobility. This is evident in the lack of analyses of downward mobility among the middle class, or upward mobility among the poor or underclass. These studies fail to acknowledge that downward mobility among the working class or middle class may have contributed to increases in the size of the underclass, or that upward mobility among the working class or underclass may have contributed to increases in the size of the middle class. Such analyses are static and unduly rigid because any discussion of vertical mobility is omitted. Phillip Bowman and Cleopatra Howard (1985) criticize the static assumptions of the underclass concept:

> Hence, the emphasis (of the "underclass") is on the pivotal role of maladaptive characteristics of black youth which are considered relatively *permanent* and not responsive to changes in the opportunity structure. . . .
>
> Perhaps the most serious limitation in the underclass position is the tendency to assume that the prevalent attitudinal, behavioral and academic problems that plague black youth are *unchangeable* and largely divorced from current racial barriers and opportunities. (Bowman and Howard 1985, 135)

## EQUATING CLASS AND CULTURE

Equating class with culture is a common flaw, as Hylan Lewis (1967) warned, in most analyses of low-income groups in the black community. Such assessments fail to distinguish between "situational adaptations" that are reactions to current circumstances, and "historical adaptations" that are cultural patterns which are transmitted intergenerationally through socialization. Charles Valentine (1968) refers to the latter when he states that most anthropologists apply the concept of culture to positive "formulas for living" that help groups to survive and advance over time--regardless of their current circumstances. According to Burton (1995), most ethnographers believe:

> . . .it is inaccurate to equate a behavioral outcome as "cultural" simply based on the aggregate incidence of its occurrence . . . .Behavioral outcomes do not necessarily represent people's values or aspirations, but may instead simply be the product of a series of events, circumstances and decisions that help people to survive in a particular environment. (Burton 1995, 154)

In order to keep the concepts of class adaptations and cultural continuities distinct, we recommend that such conditions as high levels of unemployment, underemployment, low wages, lack of education, crowded living quarters, female-headed families, crime, out-of-wedlock births, welfare dependency, etc., be operationally defined as situational class adaptations or symptoms of poverty. On the other hand, we and others (Bowman 1988; Harrison et al. 1990; McDaniel 1990) contend that such patterns as extended family networks, informal adoption, flexible family roles, religious orientation, high valuation of children, and respect for the elderly be operationally defined as cultural continuities transmitted from generation to generation--regardless of the contemporary social, economic, or political situation.

Based on these working definitions, the major distinction between class and cultural life-styles is that the former are responses to factors that affect specific social classes, while the latter are acquired values, attitudes and traditions, the responses to historical forces that are transmitted through socialization from generation to generation by membership in various racial, ethnic, or religious groups. This distinction facilitates the development of culturally sensitive public policies and programs that can be more effectively directed at dysfunctional class adaptations or life-styles, or at reinforcing and enhancing positive cultural adaptations.

## CONFUSING CLASS AND RACE

Another common practice is the confusion of class and race. This shortcoming occurs frequently in studies that focus on racial comparisons without any controls for socio-economic status. Such analyses often result in generalizations about differences between blacks and whites that are attributed to race. Most studies, for example, that compare such attributes as female-headed families or out-of-wedlock births among blacks to whites, rarely control for social class. Such comparisons are misleading because the analyses are actually comparing a mostly middle-income racial group (whites) with a mostly low-income racial group (blacks).

However, even when one attempts to match blacks and whites on socio-economic status, they are not still comparable because of the unique past and present experiences of individual and institutional racism by blacks. Billingsley (1968) observes:

> Even if two groups of white and Negro families were matched with exactly the same income, education, and occupation, they would still not be comparable. For the Negro group must reflect its experience with the caste barrier as well as its distinctive history, both of which set the conditions for growing up black in white America. (Billingsley 1968, 201)

Furthermore, it is important to recognize the diversity of values, attitudes and behaviors among groups who are in similar socio-economic levels. Many classic studies of the black poor revealed that low-income blacks are not monolithic and exhibit a wide range of values, attitudes, and child-rearing practices (Lewis 1967; Jeffers 1967; Ladner 1974).

## CONFUSING ATTRIBUTES AND CORRELATES

Another common weakness of most studies of class or culture patterns is the failure to distinguish between attributes and correlates. This fallacy often leads to tautological analyses and confuses causes, correlates, and effects. Attributes refer to the *intrinsic* traits of class or cultural life-styles, while correlates refer to their *extrinsic* characteristics. Attributes are constants, since they are integral to the definition of an adaptation or life-style. Correlates, on the other hand, are variables because they are part of a hypothesis (or outcomes) to be investigated.

Whether a characteristic is part of a definition or part of a hypothesis depends on the specific purpose of the inquiry. Traits operationally defined as attributes in one study, may be defined as correlates in another. The only condition is that they must be defined consistently throughout the *same* study. For example, when an analyst defines welfare recipiency as an attribute (or constant) of the underclass, *all* members of the underclass in that study must be on welfare. However, if another analyst defines welfare recipiency as a correlate (or variable) of the underclass, this would require that welfare recipiency *not* be used as a criterion for membership in the group to permit investigation of the proportion of those members who receive welfare as a variable. Similarly, one researcher may define an extended-family household as a cultural attribute, while another may define it as a cultural correlate.

Once Wilson (1987) defines the underclass as long-term jobless, poor, and welfare dependents who live in extreme poverty areas, those traits become class attributes that cannot vary. Consequently, it would be tautological to investigate the variation of unemployment, poverty, or welfare dependency in his analyses of the underclass, since they are constants and not variables. Similarly, since Wilson also defines working class blacks who move outside poverty areas as "stable," this prevents any analysis of the degree of stability of working class blacks who live outside poverty areas, since this attribute is constant.

Stephen Steinberg (1995, 141) summarizes this confusion of cause and effect as follows: "The issue here is not whether there is an underclass, or whether members engage in 'socially dysfunctional behavior.' Rather, the issue is whether their behavior *explains* why they are in the underclass, or, conversely, whether these individuals first find themselves in the underclass (typically as a matter of birth) and only then develop 'socially disfunctional behavior." It is important that analysts of black family life are sensitive to avoiding these common misuses of the class concept.

## RECENT CLASS TRENDS

We will now examine recent class trends among African American families. First, we will focus on trends relating to "underclass" individuals and families, and then we will examine class strata trends among black families: nonworking poor, working poor, working near-poor, middle class, and upper class.

### Underclass Trends

In order to examine in-depth a broad range of issues related to the underclass, the Social Science Research Council Committee for Research on the Urban Underclass and the Northwestern University Center for Urban Affairs and Policy Research sponsored a conference on the urban underclass in October 1989. Christopher Jencks and Paul E. Peterson edited and compiled the conference papers into the volume *The Urban Underclass.* (1991)

Jencks' very incisive essay (1991) examines recent trends to answer the question, "Is the Underclass Growing?" Although Jencks expresses a preference for the traditional sociological "lower class" over "underclass" because he fails to see qualitative differences between the two concepts, he nevertheless decides to use the latter concept in his analysis to conform to current usage. He presents data from the 1960s and 1970s to the 1980s that related to unemployment, education, poverty, welfare recipiency, out-of-wedlock births, and violent crime among low-income blacks and whites.

His analysis reveals a growth in the underclass in two areas: joblessness and out-of-wedlock births. Over the past two decades, joblessness rose among low-income men--adults and youth. Among poor black men, 25-54 years old, the proportion who did not work the entire year jumped from 2.6 percent in 1968 to 6.9 percent by 1986. Similarly, the proportion of black youth, 18-19 years old, who were idle (that is, not working, not in school, and not in the military) soared from about 15 percent in 1971 to about 24 percent in 1985.

While out-of-wedlock births among all black women jumped from 35 percent in 1969 to 63 percent in 1986, out-of-wedlock births among black women with less than nine years of education soared from 42 percent to 79 percent. Yet, it should be noted that while the proportion of out-of-wedlock births among all black women rose, their nonmarital birth rates (births per 1,000 unmarried women aged 15-44) declined from 95.5 to 80.9 between 1970 and 1986. Moreover, while the out-of-wedlock birth rates among black women aged 15-17 plummeted from 140.7 to 95.8 between 1970 and 1983, their rates rose to 112.8 by 1990.

On the other hand, Jencks' analysis reveals declines in the underclass in education, welfare recipiency, and violent crime. The proportion of school dropouts among black youth fell sharply over the past two decades. The proportion of dropouts among black youth aged 16-24 fell from 23 to 17 percent between 1970 and 1988. Moreover, the National Assessment of Educational Progress (NAEP) revealed that proficiency levels in reading, mathematics, and science of black youth between the ages of 9 and 17 rose steadily since 1970. For example, while the reading proficiency scores of 13-year old black youth jumped from 220 to 239 between 1970-71 and 1983-84, the reading scores of 17-year old black youth rose from 241 to 264. Similarly, while the math achievement scores of 13-year old black youth increased from 228 to 249 between 1972-73 and 1985-86, the math achievement scores of 17-year old black youth rose from 270 to 279 (*Child Trends* 1989).

Although the proportion of families on welfare increased during the 1970s, the rate fell sharply by the end of the 1980s. Jencks estimated that, while the proportion of all female-headed families with children who received AFDC rose from 37 to 63 percent between 1968 and 1972, the proportion of families with children on AFDC fell sharply to 45 percent by 1988. While Census Bureau data reveal much lower levels of welfare recipiency, they show somewhat similar trends among black families. While the proportion of black families on welfare rose from 18 to 24 percent between 1969 and 1979, the rate fell to 21 percent by 1989.

Contrary to conventional wisdom, Jencks' analysis reveals that the rates of violent crime among blacks have dropped steadily since 1970. While homicide rates (murders per 100,000 persons) among black males fell from 67.6 to 53.3 between 1970 and 1987, the rates of aggravated assaults among blacks declined from 226 to 168 between 1973-75 and 1985-86. Violent crime even declined among black youth. Between 1970 and 1985, homicide rates among black males aged 15-24 fell from 102.5 to 66.1. However, by 1987, homicide rates among black youth rose to 85.6.

Jencks obtained mixed results with respect to poverty trends. Although poverty among all individuals has remained about the same since 1970, poverty among all families has increased. While the number of poor black families with children rose from 1.2 million to 1.8 million between 1970 and 1989, their poverty rates remained at 35 percent during that nineteen-year span. Clearly, based on poverty data, one would have to conclude that the underclass has grown among black families over the past two decades. Jencks offers important conclusions about his findings:

> The trends I have described do not fit together in any simple or obvious way. Those who think that everything has gotten worse for people at the bottom of the social pyramid since 1970 are clearly wrong. Economic conditions have deteriorated for workers without higher education, and two-parent families have become scarcer, but welfare dependency has not increased since the early 1970's, and illiteracy, teenage motherhood, and violence have declined somewhat. . . .
>
> The illusion of class homogeneity does no harm in some contexts, but it encourages two kinds of logical error when we try to describe social change. First, whenever we observe an increase in behavior that has traditionally been correlated with membership in a particular class, we tend to assume that the class in question must be getting bigger. If more working-age men are jobless, for example, we assume that the underclass must be getting bigger, without stopping to ask whether the men who have become jobless are in fact poor or have other attributes that might make them part of the underclass. The second error is a mirror image of the first. Once we decide that a class is growing, we tend to assume that every form of behavior associated with membership in that class is becoming more common. Having concluded that the underclass is getting bigger, we assume that

dropout rates, crime and teenage parenthood must also be rising.
The underlying logic here is that if one correlate of membership
in the underclass is rising, all must be rising. (Jencks 1991, 96-97)

Many of the other papers in the volume refuted or qualified
some of Wilson's propositions about the underclass.
Reynold Farley's analysis (1991) of population changes in
metropolitan areas between 1970 and 1980 reveals virtually no
changes in the extent of economic segregation within the black (or
white) communities. Thus, his findings do not support sharp
increases in the residential separation of underclass blacks from
working class (and middle class) blacks. Additionally, Marta Tienda
and Haya Stier (1991) found that working-age adults in the poorest
neighborhoods of Chicago had a strong work ethic: most of these
adults were working or looking for work. They also found that,
contrary to popular belief, black men were much more willing than
white men to accept low-paying jobs. Clearly, these underclass
adults did not have "culture of poverty" values that involved weak
commitments toward work.

In the concluding essay of the volume, Wilson (1991) rejects the
findings of most of the papers as being irrelevant to his propositions
about the urban underclass. He contends that his conceptions about
the underclass were confined to residents of the poorest census
tracts (that is, 40 percent or more residents in poverty) who resided
in the five largest metropolitan areas.

This is a very unfortunate limitation because it reduces
markedly the significance of Wilson's theoretical propositions. In
the past, most scholars have not operationally defined the
geographical location at one point in time as an attribute of a
specific class stratum (such as the "poor" or "lower class"). Such
traits have usually been treated as correlates of class concepts.
Wilson's restriction would preclude investigation of "underclass"
patterns in rural areas, suburban areas, or small towns. Moreover,
scientific knowledge would not be advanced significantly, if one uses
a geographically defined class concept that is limited
disproportionately to specific racial and ethnic groups, such as
blacks and Hispanics, and excludes most low-income whites. Many
researchers would want to investigate or compare patterns of the
underclass among poor whites as well. Most significantly, such a

limitation would have little value for social policy because policy makers would not support the targeting of federal funds to economically distressed inner-city neighborhoods, which are primarily black and Hispanic, while excluding equally distressed low-income white communities that are outside central cities. Stephen Steinberg (1995) and Michael Katz (1993) provide enlightening critiques of the research and policy implications of a misused concept of the underclass.

We now examine trends among five class strata among blacks from 1969 to 1989: nonworking poor, working poor, working near-poor, middle class, and upper class. We use annual income as the primary criterion for classifying each of the various class strata: nonworking poor (under $15,000), working poor (under $15,000), working near-poor ($15,000-34,999), middle class ($35,000-74,999), and upper class ($75,000 and over).

## Nonworking Poor

The nonworking poor (or underclass) are families in which one or both of the heads of households have a weak attachment to the labor force because of low education levels, child-care or other household responsibilities, ill health, or an inability to obtain steady work. Most of these families are concentrated in central cities, and three out of four (77 percent) of their families are headed by women. The nonworking poor had some of the largest increases (+133%) among black families over the past two decades. The number of nonworking poor increased from 597,000 to 1,390,000 between 1969 and 1989, raising their proportion among all black families from 13 to 19 percent. A major reason for this growth was the sharp decline of workers in their families. The proportion of nonworking poor families with at least one earner fell sharply from 75 to 45 percent. Six out of ten (61 percent) nonworking poor families received public assistance. Although the heads of nonworking poor families have low educational levels, their educational attainment improved markedly over the past two decades. The proportion with less than a high school education fell sharply from 85 to 52 percent, and the proportion who finished high school rose from 13 to 35 percent.

## The Working Poor

The working poor are families in which at least one head of household has a regular attachment to the labor force. He/she usually works frequently, although usually at poverty-level wages. Eight out of ten (86 percent) of these families have one or more earners. Most working poor--both adults and youth--work at below minimum wages and more often obtain part-time jobs. They often work at unskilled or low-paying service jobs that do not provide fringe benefits. Most (74 percent) of these families are concentrated in central cities. Between 1969 and 1989, the proportion of working poor families headed by women increased from 48 to 60 percent. These families had one of the smallest rates of growth (+31 percent) of black families over the past two decades. Since the number of working poor families slowly increased from 1.1 million to 1.4 million, the proportion of working poor among all black families declined from 22 to 19 percent.

Although working poor family heads have low educational levels, their educational attainment increased markedly over the past two decades. While the proportion of working poor with less than a high school education declined sharply from 78 from 42 percent, the proportion who completed high school rose from 19 to 40 percent. As one scholar (Kim 1996) notes, most of the working poor are not marginal workers, that is, youth or the elderly. They are mainly married couples who are in their prime working years. Although many of the working poor are economically eligible for public benefits, such as food stamps, public housing, AFDC, Medicaid, etc., most of them are not public assistance recipients (Hill 1981; Kim 1996).

## Working Near-Poor

The near-poor are families in which one or more of the heads of households have a strong attachment to the labor force. Nine out of ten (96 percent) of these black families have one or more earners. These families often work in semi-skilled occupations or hold low-income service or white-collar jobs. Three out of four (77 percent) near-poor families live in central cities. The proportion of such families headed by women doubled from 20 to 42 percent over the past two decades. Near-poor families had the smallest growth (+22%) of all black families. Because the number of near-poor families increased from 2.0 million to 2.5 million between 1969 and 1989, the proportion of near-poor families declined markedly from 43 to 33 percent. The educational attainment of the near-poor rose sharply. While the proportion of near-poor family heads who did not finish high school fell from 69 to 31 percent, the proportion who completed high school rose from 25 to 44 percent.

## Middle Class

The middle class are usually families in which both household heads are in the labor force. They hold middle-income white-collar or professional occupations, often in the government sector. Although four out of five (77 percent) middle class families are headed by two parents, the proportion of middle class families headed by women doubled from 12 to 23 percent between 1969 and 1989. Contrary to popular belief, three out of five (62 percent) middle class black families live in central cities, while only two out of five (38 percent) live in suburban areas. Nevertheless, the proportion of middle class families that live in the suburbs doubled from 20 to 38 percent. Middle class black families had one of the largest increases (+86 percent) over the past two decades. While the number of middle class families almost doubled from 1.0 million to 1.9 million between 1969 and 1989, their proportion among all families rose from 21 to 25 percent. Heads of middle class families are educated, with almost half (45 percent) college educated. The proportion of middle class families with some college education rose from 19 to 45 percent between 1969 and 1989, and the proportion who completed at least four years of college rose from 9 to 19 percent. Yet, it should be clearly understood that the major criterion for attaining middle class status in most black families is to have two earners--that is, working wives (Hill et al. 1993).

## Upper Class

Upper class families are also families in which both household heads are employed. They usually occupy upper income white-collar jobs, or are executives or managers, or are professionals--often in the private sector. Although eight out of ten (82 percent) upper class families comprise two parents, the proportion of upper class families headed by women rose markedly from 2 to 16 percent between 1969 and 1989. Upper class families had the largest growth (+367 percent) of all black families. The number of upper class families increased five-fold (from 72,000 to 336,000) between 1969 and 1989, raising their proportion from 2 to 5 percent of black families (**fig. 3**). Contrary to conventional wisdom, half (50 percent) of upper-class families live in the central cities, while the remaining half live in suburbs. However, the proportion who live in the suburbs soared from 31 to 50 percent between 1969 and 1989. The heads of upper class families are educated. Seven out of ten (69 percent) had some college education, and almost half (44 percent) completed at least four years of college in 1989. Two decades earlier, in 1969, half (49 percent) of upper class families had some college education, and three out of ten (30 percent) had completed at least four years of college.

Yet, we should be careful not to exaggerate the growth of the middle and upper class among blacks because they are often not economically comparable with the white middle and upper classes (Myrdal 1941; Billingsley 1968). First, as Oliver and Shapiro (1995) and Anderson (1994) observe, most middle and upper class black families attain their status through (two) incomes and occupations, while comparable whites achieve their status through wealth and assets, which are ten times greater than blacks. Second, several observers (Duncan 1992; Reich 1994) have noted, the growth of the white middle class has slowed, and the gap between them and the white upper class has been widening. There is similar evidence that the growth in the black middle class has also slowed in recent decades (Billingsley 1992; Hill et al. 1993). Home ownership--a historic attribute of the middle class--has remained substantially the same (42 to 43 percent) among blacks between 1970 and 1990, while steadily rising (65 to 68 percent) among whites. The steady decline in scholarships and grants for black college students is likely to slow the growth of the black middle class even further during the 21st century.

**Fig. 3:  Black Class Structure, 1969-1989**

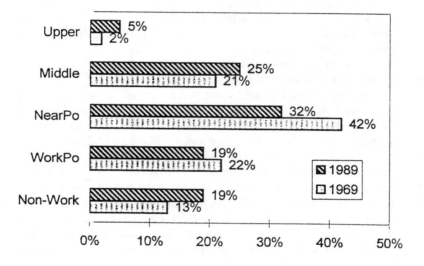

Source:          U.S. Census Bureau Current Population Survey
                 data for 1969 and 1989.

In sum, while the nonworking black poor increased from 13 to 19 percent between 1969 and 1989, the black working class (working poor and working near-poor) declined from 64 to 51 percent, and the black middle class and upper class rose from 23 to 30 percent. These findings suggest that, while 6 percent of the black working class experienced downward mobility, 7 percent of them experienced upward mobility. Additionally, three out of ten black families today are in the middle or upper class.

# Chapter 4

# Strong Achievement Orientation

African Americans have a rich legacy of achievement. As most anthropologists (including European scientists, such as George Leakey) confirm, the continent of Africa was the birthplace of man. As late as the mid-1600s, the entire continent of Africa was referred to as *Ethiopia,* a Greek word which meant sunburnt or dark-skinned people. Ethiopia was the source of the civilization of Egypt, whose original name was Kemit, meaning "people of the black land" (Browder 1989).

Despite the efforts of some scientists to "move" Egypt to the Middle East, Egypt is in Africa. African architects and mathematicians were responsible for designing the Great Pyramids (2980 B.C.-2475 B.C.) and the Sphinx in Egypt as well as magnificent pyramids in the Sudan. Egyptian civilization left the world such legacies as the calendar, mathematics, writing--the alphabet, paper, ink, pen, geography, literature, art, surgery (Karenga 1987). According to Cheikh Anta Diop (1991), many Greek scholars were educated in Egypt: Thales was the first Greek pupil of the Egyptians; Pythagoras was in Egypt for twenty-two years; and Hippocrates was taught at the Temple of Imhotep at Memphis, Egypt during the 5th century, B.C.

In addition to the earlier empires of Ethiopia and Egypt, other influential states included Ghana (A.D. 300-1240), Mali (A.D. 1230-1464), and Songhai (A.D. 1464-1591). These African civilizations had universities (especially, the University of Jenne of Timbuktu) that taught the scientific disciplines of mathematics, architecture, engineering, medicine, astronomy, botany, physics, geometry, and geography.

These achievements in science and technology continued after Africans were brought to the United States. Even during slavery, many free blacks were responsible for numerous inventions, such as, the first clock, a dry cleaning process, the corn planter, cotton planter, bed frame, a sugar refining technique, a toggle harpoon, a sailboat handling device, etc. It should also be noted that many inventions, such as, the cotton gin and steam-boat propeller, were developed by black slaves, who were not allowed to take out patents for their products (James 1989).

After emancipation, black scientists and engineers were responsible for inventing such products as automatic lubricators for steam engines, the screw press, incandescent filaments for the electric lamp, a telephone telegraph transmitter, an electromotive railway system, safety valves, and a snow-melting device, a shoe-lasting machine, bread-making and bread-crumbing machines, combination air and bed pan, a railroad-car coupler, a shoe polish formula, a hair-straightening process, a gas mask, and a traffic light.    Clearly, African Americans have made outstanding contributions to world civilization through their creativity, and innovativeness **(table 4)**.

A historical perspective is needed for the current thrust to increase the participation of blacks in the "hard" sciences. It is often forgotten that historically black colleges have a long history of preparing black students as scientists.   The first courses on electrical engineering were offered by Tuskegee Institute in the 1890s.  For decades, numerous HBCUs, such as Morgan State and others, have won national competitions in such fields as chemistry, physics, biology, etc.  It was unfortunate that many of the black graduates in the sciences were not able to find employment in their fields of study because of widespread racial discrimination.

## PARENTAL EDUCATIONAL ORIENTATION

Most research on the academic performance of black youth attempt to explain why they fail and underachieve in school, not why they succeed.  While most analysts cite disadvantaged family backgrounds (such as low income, the absence of fathers, etc.) as major contributors to black academic failure, they place major emphasis on their cultural deficits, notably, the low value placed on education by black parents and children.

Yet research studies that have actually measured the academic orientation of black parents have found them to be equal to or higher than the orientation of white parents.  The classic James Coleman (1966) study of equal educational opportunity, for

## Table 4:    Selected Inventions by Blacks

| Invention | Year | Inventor |
|---|---|---|
| The first clock | 1761 | Benjamin Banneker |
| Sailboat handle | 1800 | James Forton |
| Dry cleaning process | 1821 | Thomas Jennings |
| Corn Planter | 1834 | Henry Blair |
| Cotton Planter | 1836 | Henry Blair |
| Bedframe | 1843 | Henry Boyd |
| Sugar refining process | 1843 | Norbert Rillieux |
| Toggle whale harpoon | 1848 | Lewis Temple |
| Steamboat propeller | 1850s | Benjamin Montgomery |
| Self-lubricator cup | 1872 | Elijah McCoy |
| Screw press | 1879 | Peter Campbell |
| Light bulb filaments | 1882 | Lewis Latimer |
| Telegraph transmitter | 1887 | Granville Woods |
| "Third rail" for subways | 1888 | Granville Woods |
| Safety valves | 1890 | Frank Ferrell |
| Snow-melting devices | 1890 | Frank Ferrell |
| Shoe-lasting machine | 1891 | Jan Matzeliger |
| Bread-crumbing machine | 1895 | Joseph Lee |
| Air and bed pan | 1890s | Mrs. Clara Frye |
| Railroad car coupler | 1897 | Andrew Beard |
| Shoe polish formula | 1900 | A. C. Howard |
| Hair straightening | 1905 | Madame C. J. Walker |
| Gas mask | 1914 | Garrett Morgan |
| Traffic light signal | 1923 | Garrett Morgan |
| Air-conditioning unit | 1949 | Frederick Jones |
| Meat preservative salts | 1951 | Lloyd Hall |

Source:        James (1989)

example, found that black parents often have higher educational aspirations for their children than white parents:

> These reports, even if exaggerated, indicated that the Negro children, their parents, or both, are highly directed toward the school system as a means toward social mobility. The general pattern that the reports show, of parents highly interested in their educational success,is probably correct. It is evident, however, that this interest often does not get translated into action, which supports the child's work in school. There may be a much less simple connection than ordinarily assumed between a parent's expressed interest in educational achievement, and his behavior in providing the encouragement and aid to his child that makes high achievement possible. (Coleman 1966, 192)

Since Coleman's study, numerous scholars (Bachman 1970; Slaughter-Defoe et al. 1990; Stevenson et al. 1990) confirm the findings of the Coleman study. Walter Allen's (1976) study of youth aspirations found the parents' aspirations and expectations to be major determinants. More specifically, Allen found the aspirations of black mothers to be the strongest correlate of the mobility aspirations of their adolescent children. Unfortunately, there have been few large-scale studies that attempt to relate academic performance to academic motivation among representative cross-sections of black and white parents and children. One of those investigations was conducted by Harold Stevenson et al. (1990) among over 3,000 black, white, and Hispanic children in grades one, three and five (as well as their parents) in the metropolitan area of Chicago. When parents were asked-- without controlling for social class--to rate the importance to them of their child's getting a good grade, black and Hispanic mothers placed greater importance on their child's academic achievement than did white mothers. Similarly, black and Hispanic mothers perceived their children positive about school than white parents:

> [Most] mothers. . . .perceived their child as being positive about school, but black and Hispanic mothers portrayed even greater enthusiasm on the part of their child than did the white mothers. Hispanic and/or black mothers were more likely than white mothers to believe that their child spoke positively about the teacher, looked

forward to homework, came home from school happy, could not wait
for vacations to end, and was eager to go to school each morning.
(Stevenson et al. 1990, 515)

The Stevenson et al. (1990) study also found that higher
proportions of white (71 percent) and black (63 percent) than
Hispanic (55 percent) mothers expected their child to attend college.
The 1993 National Household Education Survey, however, found
about the same proportions of black and white parents (without
controlling for social class) expected their child to attend college: at
the 3-5 grades (97 versus 96 percent, respectively), at the 6-9th
grades (93 versus 93 percent) and at the 10-12th grades (93 versus
93 percent).   However, black parents were more likely than white
parents to expect their children to finish college--regardless of
grade: at the 3-5 grades (93 versus 90 percent), at the 6-9th grades
(87 versus 83 percent) and at the 10-12th grades (83 versus 79
percent) (National Center for Education Statistics 1995).
It is important to realize that these studies reveal that the high
educational aspirations of black parents occur at all income levels,
including poor families.    Among families with incomes under
$20,000, for example, 83 percent of black parents expect their
children to complete college, compared with 72 percent of white
parents.    Similarly, 91 percent of black parents expect their
children to attend college, compared with 86 percent of white
parents (National Center for Education Statistics 1995) **(table 5)**.
Obviously, the higher educational expectations of many low-
income black parents relative to white parents regarding college
attainment of their children will not be realized, because higher
proportions of white than black youth will actually attend and
complete college. Nevertheless, these findings confirm that one
cannot attribute the lower academic attainment of black to white
youth to the low valuation of education by their parents. Although
low-income black parents have high achievement motivation for
their children, they need support in translating their expectations
into reality.

## YOUTH EDUCATIONAL ORIENTATION

Not surprisingly, studies that have systematically assessed achievement motivation found a strong achievement orientation among low-income and middle-income African American children. Despite lower scores on standardized achievement tests of black children than white children, black children have educational and occupational aspirations that are often equal to, and sometimes higher, than white children (Stevenson et al. 1990; Winfield 1991b). Scholars (Miller and Haller 1964; Edwards 1976) have found that high aspirations are one of the strongest predictors of upward educational and occupational mobility among black youth.

The Stevenson et al. (1990) study obtained results among the elementary students that were somewhat similar among their parents. Black children had more positive attitudes toward reading, math, school and homework than white children (without controlling for class) at all three (1, 3, and 5) grade levels. Moreover, 93 percent of the fifth-grade black students expected to attend college, compared with 80 percent of the fifth-grade white students.

According to the 1993 National Household Education Survey, while the same proportion (96 percent) of black and white 6-9th graders expected to go to college, higher proportions of white (96 percent) than black (93 percent) 10-12th graders expected to attend college. While comparable proportions of black (94 percent) and white (93 percent) 6-9th graders expected to complete college, similar proportions of black (84 percent) and white (85 percent) 10-12th graders expected to complete college (National Center for Education Statistics 1995). It is also interesting to note that the declines in the expectations of youth to complete college fell between the 6-9th and 10-12th grade levels among both black and white students.

An analysis of the educational plans of seniors in the 1992 cohort of the National Education Longitudinal Study concluded:

There are no differences between black and white seniors in their plans for postsecondary education. Approximately equal proportions

## Table 5

A.  **Educational Expectations of Parents of 6–12th Graders by Race and Income, 1993**

| Educational Expectations | Under $20,000 | | | $40,000 and Over | | |
|---|---|---|---|---|---|---|
| | Black | White | Diff. | Black | White | Diff. |
| Graduate HS | 97% | 97% | 0 | 99% | 100% | -1% |
| Go to College | 91% | 86% | +5 | 96% | 97% | -1% |
| Finish College | 83% | 72% | +11 | 90% | 89% | +1% |

B.  **Educational Expectations of 6–12th Graders by Race and Income, 1993**

| Educational Expectations | Under $20,000 | | | $40,000 and over | | |
|---|---|---|---|---|---|---|
| | Black | White | Diff. | Black | White | Diff. |
| Graduate HS | 100% | 99% | +1 | 100% | 100% | 0 |
| Go to College | 92% | 90% | +2 | 97% | 98% | -1 |
| Finish College | 86% | 80% | +6 | 94% | 93% | +1 |

Source:  Analyses conducted by author from U.S. Department of Education, National Center for Education Statistics, 1993 National Household Education Survey Public Use Data.

of black (62%) and white (63%) seniors intend to continue their
education at a four-year college.
(Office of Educational Research and Improvement 1995, 78)

Low-income black youth often have higher educational
attainment and aspirations than low-income white youth. Poor
blacks are more likely to graduate from high school than poor
whites (Slaughter-Defoe et al. 1990). Furthermore, among students
in grades 6-12 from families with incomes under $20,000, 86 percent
of the black youth expect to complete college, compared with 80
percent of white youth. Similarly, 92 percent of low-income black
youth expect to go to college, compared with 90 percent of low-
income white youth (National Center for Education Statistics 1995)
**(table 5)**.

The Coleman (1966) study also revealed higher educational
aspirations among black than white children. Analysts who have
been puzzled by these findings sought to explain them in terms of
pathology. They concluded that these aspirations were "too high"
and "unrealistic" for black children, and that these lofty goals
should be lowered to prevent black children from becoming
frustrated in later life. Indeed, many "misguidance" counselors
often lower the aspirations of black children to such an extent that
the children lose interest in schooling, and begin to drop out in
large numbers.

Moreover, studies have shown that teachers can lower the
academic performance of children by having lower expectations for
them based on their race or social class. In an experiment
conducted by two researchers (Rosenthal and Jacobson, 1968),
teachers were told that one group of young elementary students
were "spurters," and the other group were "slower" learners. The
students had been tested in advance, and they were randomly
assigned to both groups. Although both groups had similar
achievement scores, the teachers were informed that they were
unequal achievers. Eight months later both groups were retested.
Researchers found that the children who had been labeled *slow*
learners achieved lower IQ gains than the children who had been
labeled *spurters.* The analysts concluded that the teachers
unconsciously lowered their expectations for the "slower" children,
and raised their expectations for the "spurters."

These results confirm a negative self-fulfilling prophecy: although these students started out as equal achievers, their subsequent differential performance resulted from different teacher expectations based on the labels they had been assigned. Unfortunately, in many classrooms across the nation, teachers' expectations of students are more determined by race or class than by their actual abilities or potentialities. Lower teacher expectations may play a major role in the decline in the academic motivation of black youth as they enter higher grades (Rosenberg and Simmons 1972; Stevenson et al. 1990). Janice Hale-Benson (1982) and Lisa Delpit (1995) provide enlightening critiques of culturally insensitive practices in the classroom that impede the educational attainment of children of color.

## PEER APPROVAL OF ACHIEVEMENT

According to conventional wisdom, black students are more likely than white students to have peers who disapprove of academic achievement and hard work in school. According to some ethnographic research (Fordham and Ogbu 1986; Fordham 1988), many black youth are reputed to disparage high achieving peers as "acting white." Yet, data from national studies reveal that most black students are just as supportive, and sometimes more, of academic achievement by their peers as white students.

Based on the 1992 cohort of the National Education Longitudinal Survey, 56 percent of black seniors said that their close friends felt that it was "very important" that they get good grades, compared with 47 percent of white seniors. Similarly, 55 percent of black seniors said that their peers felt it was "very important" to attend classes regularly, compared with 50 percent of white seniors (Office of Educational Research and Improvement 1995). Moreover, the 1993 Household Education Survey revealed that comparable proportions of black (86 percent) and white (89 percent) students in grades 6-12 said their peers felt that hard work to get good grades was "very or somewhat important."

These data also reveal that the peers of low-income blacks are almost as supportive of good grades and proper behavior as middle-income blacks. Eighty-three percent of black youth from families with incomes under $20,000 said that their friends approve of hard work to get good grades, compared with 89 percent of black youth from families with $40,000 or more incomes. Similarly, 75 percent of black youth from families with income under $20,000 said that their friends approve of their exhibiting good behavior in school, compared with 79 percent of black youth from families with $40,000 or more incomes (National Center for Education Statistics 1995). These data demonstrate that, contrary to conventional wisdom, the overwhelming majority of low-income black youth have peers who are supportive of academic achievement (U.S. Department of Health and Human Services 1996).

## SELF-ESTEEM

Many studies have also revealed that high self-esteem is strongly correlated with subsequent achievement orientation and upward mobility. Yet, it interesting that many researchers (Kardiner and Ovesey 1951; Proshansky and Newton 1968) merely assumed, without conducting any specific studies that measured this concept, that blacks had lower self-esteem than whites. These assumptions were based on the erroneous belief that because blacks experience prejudice and discrimination, they must have high levels of self-hatred and low levels of self-esteem.

However, researchers (Powell and Fuller 1973; Hurstfield 1978; Simmons 1978) who conducted more reliable empirical studies found that self-esteem among blacks was more often equal to and sometimes higher than self-esteem among whites. In fact, based on large representative samples of black and white children in an urban community, Morris Rosenberg and Roberta Simmons (1972) found self-esteem to be consistently higher among blacks than whites. Moreover, the authors conducted a comprehensive review of twelve studies on self-esteem. Their review showed that eight of the studies found higher levels of self-esteem among black than white children.

A recent review of studies of self-esteem among blacks of all ages by Sandra Nettles and Joseph Pleck (1994) found that blacks and whites had comparable levels of self-esteem. The authors revealed that the attitude of significant others (parents, peers, and teachers) toward the child was an important source of self-esteem among black children (Taylor 1976; Gibbs 1985). They concluded, "Thus, the evidence does not suggest that low self-esteem is a risk factor of particular importance for African American youths. . . ." (Nettles and Pleck 1994, 163).

## RACIAL IDENTITY

Interestingly, the early studies of self-esteem among blacks that were conducted during the 1940s, 1950s, and 1960s actually focused on racial identity. For example, the classic studies of Kenneth and Mamie Clark (1947) showed black children dolls of different colors to determine their racial preferences. Other researchers used projective techniques (including dolls, pictures, drawings, puppets, etc.) to assess the racial identity of black children. Most of these studies found that black children more often preferred the white or light-skinned dolls or pictures. Based on these results, the researchers concluded that these findings revealed high levels of self-hatred and low levels of self-esteem.

Even when researchers used direct measures or attitude scales of racial preferences, they often made inferences and conclusions about self-hatred, although they rarely used direct measures of personal identity or self-esteem. In a comprehensive review of eighteen empirical racial preference studies that are most often cited for documenting black self-hatred between 1939 and 1960, William Cross, Jr., (1985) found that seventeen of these studies only had measures of group, not personal, identity. He concluded that these investigators erroneously assumed that reference group preference is an appropriate proxy for personal identity.

A reexamination of thirty-two racial preference studies by W. C. Banks (1976) suggests that their forced choice techniques obscure the extent of biculturalism among blacks by constraining them to select "no one group preference" as a proxy for "both group preferences." Blacks indicated no preference (that is, a preference for cultural symbols of *both* racial groups) in 69 percent of the studies, a preference for black symbols in 25 percent, and a preference for white symbols in the remaining 6 percent. These findings are reinforced by Cross's (1982) longitudinal study of socialization practices, which revealed that black parents were much more likely than white parents to provide their children with a multiracial world view and reference groups. Consequently, Cross

(1985) contends that pro-white preferences of blacks should not be construed as self-hatred but as manifesting racial pluralism, biculturalism, and dualism:

> Tentative results from a longitudinal study (Cross, 1982) show black parents present both the black and white worlds to their children, while white parents tend to convey the world as being primarily white. For example, in black homes, one is likely to find white dolls or human figures as well as black ones, while black dolls are seldom, if ever, found in white homes. Black children, and perhaps black people in general, have a dual reference group orientation. (Cross 1985, 169)

Moreover, Cross (1991) observes that, although the early studies of self-hatred among blacks were based largely on the racial preferences of black preschool children, the researchers had no hesitation in making broad generalizations about the "pervasive" self-hatred among black adults! In addition to underscoring the importance of including samples of blacks over a wider age span, Cross (1991) contends that appropriate scientific studies of self-concept should incorporate measures of both personal identity and group identity. Since most of the studies with measures of both personal identity and racial group identity reveal that they vary independently, it is unwarranted to make inferences about one concept from the other one.

Such a study was conducted by Harriette McAdoo (1985), who administered measures of self-esteem and racial group preferences to black children in 1969 when they were four and five years old, and again when they were ages nine and ten. Her sample included low-income and middle-income children from several northern cities and a black town in Mississippi. Although her first wave of data revealed high self-esteem among all of the children, they tended to have an out-group (pro-white) orientation. Children from two-parent, middle-class families were the most out-group oriented, although their self-esteem was equal to or higher than that of children from lower-income families. When McAdoo readministered her measures in 1975, she found that self-esteem remained high among the children, although their racial group preferences became more in-group oriented. Cross (1985) emphasizes the important contribution of McAdoo's longitudinal study:

> McAdoo's study is significant because it also showed that black children from a variety of home environments and regions of the country had high self-esteem before and after being influenced by the Black Power Movement. The same children had a predominantly out-group orientation before the Black Power Movement and an increasingly in-group orientation as the Black Power Movement progressed. (Cross 1985, 165-66)

## LOCUS OF CONTROL

Another concept that is strongly correlated with a strong achievement orientation is the nature of one's locus of control. Most studies of whites have found that an external oriented locus of control is correlated with high aspirations, and high achievement and self-esteem, while an internal orientation is correlated with low aspirations, and low achievement and self-esteem. According to J. B. Rotter (1964), internal control represents a person's belief that one's attainments in life are determined mainly by one's own behavior. Conversely, external control represents a person's belief that one's life attainments are determined by forces outside of one's control.

Many researchers have explained the lower achievement of blacks as a result of an external locus of control. Yet, few studies have tested systematically the relationship between their external orientation and achievement orientation among blacks. Patricia Gurin et al. (1969) argue that an external orientation may have positive consequences for blacks who attribute their failure to achieve to racial discrimination and not to internal deficiencies. Thus, they contend that an external orientation among blacks may be positively correlated with high self-esteem and strong achievement orientation. Accordingly, Gurin et al. (1969) observe:

> Instead of depressing motivation, focusing on external forces may be motivationally healthy if it results from assessing one's chances for success against systematic and real external obstacles, rather than the exigencies of an overwhelming, unpredictable fate.
> (Gurin et al. 1969, 33)

Patricia Gurin and Daniel Katz's (1966) study of black college students revealed that two additional measures--personal control and control ideology--were more strongly correlated with achievement orientation than J. B. Rotter's Internal-External Control scale. Personal control refers to individuals' beliefs about capacities to exercise control over their own lives, while control ideology connotes beliefs about the role of internal and external forces in the distribution of rewards in society. Thus, Gurin et al. (1969) observe:

> In the performance area, we find that the two control measures, the personal and the ideological, work in opposite ways. Students who are strongly internal in the personal sense have higher achievement test scores, achieve higher grades in college, and perform better on an anagrams task which was included in the instruments administered in the study. In contrast, students who are strongly internal in the sense of believing that internal forces are the major determinants of success in the culture at large (ideological) perform less well than the more externally-oriented students. Given that these opposing results from the two types of control measures cancel each other, the total Rotter score understandably bears no relationship to these performance indicators. (Gurin et al. 1969, 43-44)

Beverly Hendrix-Wright (1981) also conducted a study that tested the Gurin thesis by examining relationships between locus of control, self-esteem, and racial group identity among black and white high school students. She confirmed this thesis by finding that, among black students, high self-esteem was strongly correlated with internal orientation on personal control and external orientation on control ideology. Thus, she concluded:

> Thus, [black] students in this study who were high in personal control were more realistic about their occupational goals and were generally more external in their (generalized) orientation. It may be that a generally external orientation, accompanied by an internal orientation on the personal control measures the healthiest adjustment to a discriminatory environment. . . .
> It was expected that black youths who were high in racial group identification and also external in their general orientation would be highest in self-esteem and vis-a-vis those black youths who were low in racial group identification and also internal in their orientation

would be lowest in self-esteem.  This assumption was supported
by. . . . [our]. . . .research findings. (Hendrix-Wright 1981, 19-20).

Phillip Bowman and Cleopatra Howard (1985) further underscored the role of proactive socialization by black parents in
enhancing the personal control of their children that helped them
to overcome racial barriers in the external environment.  These
researchers found that black youth who attained academic success
were most likely to have internalized proactive racial orientations
from their parents that enhanced their personal sense of efficacy
over external obstacles.  These proactive orientations resulted from
parents who regularly placed major emphasis on awareness of
racial barriers and blocked opportunities, ethnic pride, self-
development, achievement ethic, human equality, and expanding
opportunities.

In sum, these findings reveal that, among black youth, a strong
achievement orientation is strongly correlated with high self-esteem,
strong racial group identity, internal personal control, external
ideological orientation, and parents who inculcate strong
educational and occupational aspirations, and proactive racial
orientations.

## BLACK COLLEGES: STILL A LIFELINE

One of the most important institutions for reinforcing the strong
achievement orientation among blacks is the historically black
college and university (HBCU).  These institutions have provided
access to college opportunities to thousands of racially
disadvantaged young people and have transformed them into
doctors, lawyers, engineers, scientists, accountants, and other
productive citizens.  HBCUs have produced the majority of black
professionals.  They have been responsible for 75 percent of all
blacks with doctoral degrees, 85 percent of all black physicians, 80
percent of all black federal judges, 75 percent of all black military
officers, 60 percent of all black attorneys, 50 percent of all black
engineers, and 48 percent of all black business executives (Warden
1996).

Although enrollment in HBCUs comprise only two percent of
college students in all American colleges and universities, they

comprise 17 percent of all black students who attend college. Moreover, HBCUs accounted for 27 percent of all baccalaureate degrees conferred on blacks in 1989-90, 15 percent of the master's degrees, 13 percent of the doctorates, and 16 percent of the first professional degrees. Overall, they awarded 17 percent of all the degrees received by blacks (NCES 1992). Moreover, 50 percent of black faculty in research universities obtained their bachelor's degree from an HBCU. While 70 percent of blacks in HBCUs complete their studies, about 70 percent of blacks in other institutions do not finish.

Enrollment in most HBCUs has been increasing, while enrollment in many other institutions of higher education has been declining. Because the growth in the number of people of color will increase sharply in the twenty-first century, these institutions need more, not less, resources to provide the quality of education that is needed to meet the demands of a complex and changing society.

## RESILIENT PROGRAMS

Fortunately, there are numerous examples of programs across this country that try to reinforce the achievement orientation of low-income children of color. The Head Start program, which was established as a War on Poverty program during the 1960s, is the most popular example of such programs. The continuing success of this preschool program is due to many factors: (a) high teacher expectation of all children regardless of race or class; (b) encouraging the active participation of the children's parents; and (c) reinforcing the high aspirations of the parents for their children. As a result of its innovative approach, evaluations of the Head Start program demonstrate that it has been especially effective in improving the academic readiness and educational and occupational aspirations of low-income children.

Another effective educational program for black youth is College Here We Come with the goal of increasing college opportunities for young people who reside in public housing. This effort was launched in 1974 by Kimi Gray and other residents of the Kenilworth-Parkside public housing development in South East Washington, D.C. It has provided a broad range of social and economic support to help more than six hundred low-income youth to attend college.

Also in Washington, D.C., PROJECT 2000 is an example of an early intervention program designed to enhance the academic performance of black boys, especially those from families headed by women. Dr. Spencer Holland, an African American educator, created this program, in collaboration with Concerned Black Men, to counteract the so-called fourth grade syndrome: the alienation of black boys from school as they reach the fourth grade. In order to provide positive male role models in the primary grades, Dr. Holland recruited adult men to volunteer as teacher assistants in grades one through three in an elementary school. This project, under the sponsorship of Morgan State University, was expanded to three elementary schools in Baltimore, Maryland. Evaluations of this program reveal that this program had positive effects in raising the academic achievement of the children (Institute for Urban Research 1993).

SIMBA ("young lion" in Swahili) is a comprehensive male-socialization program developed by Jawanza Kunjufu in Chicago, Illinois to prepare black boys between the ages of 7 and 19 for the rites of passage to responsible manhood and fatherhood. This program portrays black adult men in positive roles, develops life skills, enhances racial and cultural identity, raises self-esteem and academic performance, and promotes healthy male-female relationships. Similar rites of passage programs--for girls and boys---have been developed in numerous other cities across the nation.

# Chapter 5

---

# STRONG WORK ORIENTATION

African Americans are a work-oriented people. It is the only group in America that worked 250 years for free! After the end of slavery, blacks worked full-time for part-time pay. Most accounts of blacks focus on the minority who are unemployed or on welfare and not on the overwhelming majority who are in the work force. It is interesting how few research studies have been conducted on the black working poor (persons who work at arduous, back-breaking, and hazardous jobs for long hours at low pay), such as domestics, laundry women, charwomen, porters, cooks, laborers, maids, butlers, drivers, and farm workers (Gilkes 1980; Dill 1980; Lewis and Looney 1983). Many women who worked as servants in the homes of wealthy whites, in addition to cleaning and cooking, often had major responsibility for raising the children of their employers as well as their own. Bonnie Dill's (1980) study of black domestic workers underscored their ability to balance the work obligations of their employers, while encouraging high educational achievement for their children. Elizabeth Clark-Lewis (1994), for example, recounts the varied experiences of eighty-one women who migrated from the rural South at the turn of century to work as domestic workers in Washington, D.C.

It is often forgotten, that as late as 1960, two out of five or 2.2 million blacks in the U.S. were household servants, laborers, or farm workers. The role models for the majority of blacks during the '40s and '50s were working-class individuals who worked in low-wage service and unskilled occupations. Thus, as Bart Landry (1987) and other scholars note, the bulk of our current judges, lawyers, doctors, scientists, college professors, teachers, business persons, registered nurses, etc., were reared, socialized or influenced by parents, relatives, and friends who held low-paying occupations.

Another myth about blacks is their alleged lack of a business tradition. Yet, the history of America reveals that blacks owned numerous businesses that catered to white or black patrons--even during slavery. George Washington, as a military leader, often held meetings at Fraunces Tavern, an establishment in New York City owned by Samuel Fraunces, a free black, during the 1790s. James Horton (1979) observes that many prominent figures, such as U.S. Senator Charles Sumner, participated in numerous debates with blacks and abolitionists in John Smith's barbershop, which was used regularly for meetings and forums, in Boston during the 1850s.

Other black-owned barbershops, cleaning shops, dry goods stores, taverns, restaurants, etc., also served as important meeting places for all segments of the black Boston community during the antebellum period (Horton 1979). Thomas Jennings, a free black, operated one of the first black-owned dry cleaning and tailoring businesses in New York City during the 1820s (James 1989). Thomas Downing owned Downing's Oyster House, a popular restaurant in New York City, from 1820 to 1866 (Harris 1968).

Numerous free blacks who were skilled artisans and inventors established businesses as tailors, carpenters, furniture makers, blacksmiths, millers, carpenters, potters, coopers, printers, silversmiths, goldsmiths, architects, engineers, and electricians (Berry and Blassingame 1982). James Forten, for example, who became very proficient in the maritime trades, established a sailmaking business in 1830 after inventing a sail-handling device. After the Civil War, one of the largest shipyards in the nation, the Chesapeake Marine Railway and Dry Dock Company, was operated by a black firm at Fells Point in Baltimore for almost twenty years: 1866-84 (Thomas 1974). In fact, a black "Wall Street," with numerous thriving black businesses, existed in Tulsa, Oklahoma during the early 1900s. Unfortunately, this black business community was completely destroyed in 1921 by firebombs from the air and the ground and a pogrom spearheaded by the Ku Klux Klan (Ellsworth 1982; Wilson and Wallace 1992).

In addition, as James Hagy (1978) reminds us, many of the early black businesses during and after slavery were owned by women. Some of the most notable black women entrepreneurs included: Mary Washington, who operated a fruit and vegetable shop in New York City for thirty years during the early 1800s (Harris 1968); Ida B. Wells Barnett, newspaper publisher in Memphis during the 1890s; Maggie Lena Walker, who founded the first woman-owned bank in the nation, the St. Luke Penny Savings Bank, in 1903, in Richmond, Virginia (Ploski and Williams 1983); and Madame C. J.

Walker, who founded in 1910, in Indianapolis, the first major company in cosmetology for blacks (Bundles 1991). By 1900, the proliferation of black businesses in a wide range of fields, such as manufacturing, catering, banking, insurance and publishing, led to the formation of the National Negro Business League by Booker T. Washington.

## WORK ETHIC

A popular misconception is the belief that blacks and low-income groups have a low work ethic and prefer to go on welfare rather than to work. Yet, study after study continues to reveal that the overwhelming majority of low-income people, including welfare recipients, prefer work over welfare (Kaplan and Tausky 1972; Goodwin 1983; Rank 1994b).

Another indication of a strong work ethic is the large number of poor people who do not receive any welfare. Although one out of four black families were poor in 1989, only two out of ten received public assistance. Moreover, half (52 percent) of the officially poor black families in 1989 received no public assistance, or, 808,000 of the 1.5 million black families below the poverty level were not on welfare. Researchers have rarely conducted studies to determine why so many black families that are economically eligible for welfare do not receive any cash assistance. Several studies reveal that many of these families refuse to apply for welfare because of their strong emphasis on self-reliance and their antipathy toward welfare (Kim 1996).

Moreover, black women who head families are more work-oriented today than they were two decades ago. Between 1970 and 1990, the proportion of female heads of families in the official labor force jumped from 50 percent to 63 percent. Unfortunately, this strong work ethic was not translated into actual jobs, since the jobless rates of black female heads of families in 1990 (14.3 percent) was about three times higher than their jobless rates two decades ago (5.6 percent).

A major reason for the economic stability of many two-parent black families is the presence of working wives. Historically, a higher proportion of black wives have worked than white wives. In 1990, 66 percent of black wives in two-parent families were working compared with 57 percent of white wives. Moreover, black families with working wives have incomes ($40,038) that are twice as large as the incomes of families without working wives ($20,333).

Another popular belief is that black youth have high unemployment rates because they refuse to accept low-paying jobs. Yet many systematic studies of the work orientation of youth contradict such beliefs (Goodwin 1983; Tienda and Stier 1991). In an in-depth study that compared the work attitudes of black and white youth, Michael Borus (1980) found that black youth were much more willing to accept low-paying jobs than white youth.

Many studies of the work attitudes of low-income blacks reveal a strong commitment to work. To test the work ethic of the poor, H. Roy Kaplan and Curt Tausky (1972) interviewed 275 long-term unemployed persons, who were 62 percent black, 24 percent Hispanic, and 14 percent white. In response to the question, "If you were out of work, which would you rather do?," seventy-one percent said they would take a job as a car washer that paid the same as welfare, while only 29 percent said they would collect welfare. The respondents indicated similar preferences for work to other questions. Tom Larson (1988) summarized similar findings:

Anthropologist Oscar Lewis (1968) argued, on the basis of his work in Mexico, that a culture of poverty tends to perpetuate itself; poor people stay poor because they lack middle-class values, aspirations, and behavior. Today, some people just agree with Piore (1979) that blacks are unwilling to take menial jobs or low wages. The widening employment gap can then be attributed to changes in expectations and attitudes among blacks, due to the civil rights movement and an increase in black pride. However, actual studies have found that blacks are more willing than whites to work. This was found in a 1970 study by Hamel, Goldberg, and Gavett and in a more recent study by Borus (1980). Borus found black youth willing to work at menial jobs at lower wages than white or Hispanic youth. This tends to refute the culture of poverty theory. We do not need to resort to disparaging the victims for lack of other solutions to the youth employment problem. (Larson 1988, 118-19)

To test the extent of "shiftlessness" or low work ethic in inner-city areas, Marta Tienda and Haya Stier (1991) examined the work attitudes and behavior of parents who were black, white, Puerto

Rican, and Mexican and lived in poverty areas of Chicago. The researchers classified their respondents into four groups: the unemployed (that is, actively looking for work), the discouraged (that is, want work, but not actively seeking it), the constrained (that is, unavailable for work due to illness, handicap, child-care or family responsibilities), and the shiftless (that is, not interested in working and preference for public support). Their analysis revealed that only about six percent of inner-city parents were considered to be "potentially shiftless." Moreover, they found black men much more willing than white men to accept low-wage jobs:

> Our supplementary tabulations also showed that the average wage rate expected by those who had worked and wanted a job was $5.50 an hour for black men, $6.20 for Mexican and Puerto Rican men, and $10.20 for white men. Black men appeared most willing and white men least willing to accept low-paying jobs. (Tienda     and Stier 1991, 143)

## DISCOURAGED WORKERS

Many studies reveal that numerous persons who are not counted in the official labor force because they are no longer actively looking for work, in fact, want to work. Most of these "discouraged workers" are disproportionately black and female. Yet the Labor Department definition sharply understates the actual number of discouraged workers due to restrictive criteria.

Usually, about one-tenth of all persons outside the official labor force say they want a regular job, but only one out of five give reasons that fit the official criteria for discouraged workers. In other words, over 80 percent of all people who want work but do not look for it are excluded from the discouraged worker category. They are excluded because of unwarranted assumptions about their unavailability for work based on reasons they give for not looking. They are never explicitly asked whether they are available for work. Thus, women who say they want work but are not actively seeking it because of child-care or other family responsibilities are automatically excluded from the Labor Department's classification of discouraged workers.

In order to demonstrate the strong work commitment of women outside the official labor force, Frank Furstenberg, Jr., and Charles Thrall (1975) examined data from the National Longitudinal Survey of Women between the ages of 30 and 44 at two intervals in time-- 1967 and 1969. In 1967, the women were asked, "If you were offered a job by some employer in this area, do you think you would take it?" About one-third of the women interviewed said that they would definitely or probably accept a job if one were offered to them.

Follow-up interviews with these women in 1969 revealed that about one-third of the women who said that they were definitely available for work in 1967 were actually working two years later, as were one-fourth of the women who said they were available with qualifications. At the same time, about half of the officially unemployed women who were looking for work in 1967 were also working in 1969. On the other hand, only 15 percent of the women who reported that they were not available for work in 1967 were working two years later. Women who said they were available for work but were not looking were twice as likely to be in the labor force two years later as those who said they were not available for work. In short, the available women more closely resembled women in the official unemployed than they did the unavailable women. Furstenberg and Thrall concluded that the available women, who were not actively seeking work, should be classified with the discouraged workers, since they were ready to go to work. In order to give greater consideration to the "hidden unemployed," in 1993, the U.S. Bureau of Labor Statistics expanded its definition of the unemployed to include a subgroup of discouraged workers (Hershey 1993).

## RESILIENT PROGRAMS

Numerous grassroots groups across the nation have developed innovative efforts to reduce welfare dependency among blacks. Some of the most spectacular efforts have come from residents of public housing developments. Many of these groups have formed resident management corporations that have demonstrated that they can maintain safe, pleasant, and drug-free living environments more efficiently and cost effectively than local housing authorities.

In the Kenilworth-Parkside public housing complex in Washington, D.C., the residents have formed several small businesses, such as catering, tailoring, barbering, beauty care, thrift shops, and even a reverse commuting service to enhance the access of inner-city residents to work in suburban communities. They have hired former welfare recipients as maintenance workers to do plumbing, carpentry, and other skilled work.

As a result of tenant management, there has been a sharp decline in welfare dependence, unemployment, teenage pregnancy, school dropouts, and drug trafficking, while building repairs and rent collections have risen, indicating a sharp increase in neighborhood stability. Other successful public housing efforts abound throughout the nation, including: Jamaica Plains, Massachusetts; Cochran Gardens in St. Louis, Missouri; B. W. Cooper in New Orleans, Louisiana; and A. Henry Moore Houses in Jersey City, New Jersey.

Operation Life, founded by former welfare recipient Ruby Duncan, is another community-based development corporation that has increased business and employment opportunities for the hard-core unemployed among blacks in Las Vegas, Nevada. The Dade Women's Welfare Coalition is developing day-care centers and food cooperatives to enhance employment options for welfare recipients in Miami, Florida.

STEP-UP, an innovative program funded by the U.S. Department of Housing and Urban Development, has been established in Baltimore by the city's Housing and Community Development Department under the progressive leadership of Daniel Henson, III, HCD Commissioner. This program gives preference to: (a) hiring and training public housing residents to assist in the rehabilitation of their developments; and (b) using minority businesses as contractors in such renovation. It has been very effective in helping many public housing residents to leave the welfare rolls by enhancing their marketable skills and employability.

In order to counteract the disproportionate involvement of black youth in drug trafficking, several programs have been launched to enhance the entrepreneurial skills of inner-city youth in legal pursuits. The Educational Training and Enterprise Center (ED-TEC) in Camden, New Jersey has helped hundreds of low-income youth in many cities to create businesses in such areas as food vending, maintenance, security, and sales. A former police officer has created a mini-mall at Woodson J. H. S. in Washington, D.C. with about ten small businesses that are operated by junior high students.

Another innovative youth entrepreneurship program was designed for at-risk middle-school and high-school students by Student Achievers Future Entrepreneurs (SAFE), an African American firm located in Baltimore, Maryland. A major objective of this program is to provide inner-city youth with positive business alternatives to selling drugs. During the summers of 1995 and 1996, SAFE implemented a seven-week program, sponsored by Morgan State University's Family Life Center, to enhance entrepreneurial skills among high-risk youth 12-19 years old. In 1995, the youth set up mock businesses, developed slogans, and prepared and presented their business and marketing plans. They also designed business logos and applied the logos on T-shirts after learning the silkscreening and imprinting processes. In 1996, the youth formed a business, "Raw Dough," and marketed and sold large quantities of their products at various community events.

# Chapter 6

## Flexible Family Roles

An important African-derived cultural strength is the flexibility of family roles. In African American families, mothers often perform many traditional roles of fathers, fathers often assume customary female roles, and children perform some parental functions for younger siblings (Malson 1983; Jarrett 1994). Some social scientists have characterized black fathers who perform traditional women household chores, such as cooking, cleaning, and child care, as "henpecked" by matriarchs. Yet, such role adaptability has contributed to the stability and advancement of numerous black families. Mary Frances Berry and John Blassingame (1982) have remarked on this strength:

> After slavery, the extended family was prevalent in the black community. Generally, black households had twice as many relatives outside the immediate family as did white ones. Egalitarian in nature, the family was marked by flexibility of roles, informal adoption of children, and care for the aged. Blacks seemed to have greater abhorrence of institutionalizing the aged than whites did. When aged blacks did not live with their children, several other members of the local community took responsibility for them. (Berry and Blassingame 1982, 85)

Berry and Blassingame also stress the various strengths of black low-income and single-parent families as follows:

> The lower-class family was strong in many respects. Since it was an extended family, it had a closeness of kin missing among whites. Consider illegitimacy, for example. An illegitimate birth among blacks brought the family closer together to care for the infant; among whites, it tended to pull the family apart. In New York City in 1930, while 73 percent of black illegitimate children were in a home with the mother and her relatives, only 34 percent of white illegitimate children were in this position. Studies in the 1930's also showed that black fathers of illegitimate children were

more likely to contribute to their support than white fathers of the same class. The black woman who headed these families were the true heroines of America. Although when they worked they received considerably less money than white women did, they tended to provide better care for their children than did white women heading families. Consistently, white children were more likely to be abused or neglected than blacks in these families. In 1960, for example, only 8.4 percent of all children in institutions for dependent and neglected children in America were black. One study in 1967 showed that while 63 percent of white welfare families neglected or abused their children, only 43 percent of black welfare families did. (Berry and Blassingame 1982, 85-86)

Diane Lewis (1975) attributes the role flexibility of black families to less sex-specific socialization patterns for male and female children:

In the community Young (1970) studied there is, from a Euro-American perspective, a remarkable degree of overlap in the behavior considered appropriate for men and women. Behavior which is associated with the male role in Euro-American culture is associated with both males and females in this community. For example, females as well as males are viewed as individualistic and non-conforming in their behavior. Both husband and wife have authority in the home; both are responsible for the economic support of the family; both take the initiative in forming and breaking up a marriage and both may find separation to their advantage. (Lewis 1975, 229-30)

While we emphasize the positive consequences of flexible family roles, we must also be aware of possible dysfunctional effects. Nancy Boyd-Franklin (1989) warns social workers and therapists to be sensitive to "role confusion," in which extreme role flexibility creates stress and hostility in families. One example of this confusion is the "parental child," in which a parent completely abdicates responsibility or places unreasonable burdens for rearing young siblings on older siblings. Another example is the "nonevolved grandmother," in which tension and hostility occurs because the grandmother is not able to evolve into the grandmother's role and must assume an unreasonable burden as the surrogate mother to her grandchildren. Such circumstances often lead to role overload and burnout, especially when the grandmother (or great-grandmother) is elderly (Burton 1992; Burton 1995). To contribute to healthy family functioning, role flexibility must manifest an appropriate balance in shared parenting and in the division of household responsibilities among family members.

## EGALITARIAN FAMILY ROLES

Despite being depicted as "matriarchal," research studies of two-parent black families reveal that they are characterized by "egalitarian" patterns, or a sharing of family roles. Husbands in many black families perform various household tasks, such as cooking, child care, laundering, etc. Clearly, black wives share work responsibilities since they are in the paid labor force in two-thirds of black couples. Based on an in-depth analysis by University of Michigan researchers of the National Survey of Black Americans (NSBA), Shirley Hatchett (1991) concluded:

> Overall, there was a great deal of support for an egalitarian division of family tasks and responsibilities among the respondents in our study. More than 88% of women and men agreed (both "strongly agree" and "agree") that men and women should share in child care and household tasks and more than 98% agreed that blacks should spend more time raising their children. Three out of every four black Americans also feel that both men and women should have jobs to support the family. . . .
>
> Support for the egalitarian division of labor within the family did not differ by socioeconomic level for men. . . .[But] women with at least 16 years of education were more liberal in their attitudes than women with less education. . . .
>
> In sum, these data further document the existence of a great deal of support for egalitarianism among black Americans-both men and women. (Hatchett 1991, 90, 92)

Similarly, an analysis of national survey data by Herbert Hyman and John Reed (1969) concluded that an egalitarian patterns was the modal pattern for most black two-parent families. They found virtually no difference between the responses about family decision-making among blacks and whites.

## RESILIENCE OF SINGLE PARENT FAMILIES

Role flexibility is most evident in the disproportionate number of African American families headed by women. According to conventional wisdom, single-parent families headed by women are depicted as "broken," while two-parent families are described as "intact." However, such characterizations erroneously equate family structure with family functioning. The extent of disorganization of families depends of the quality of their functioning in various domains, not on their structure. Moreover, since single-parent families differ widely depending on the composition, age, and marital status of the household head, number and age of children, support networks, work experience, etc., the effectiveness of their functioning also varies. Several research studies have revealed that many one-parent families are more intact or cohesive than many two-parent families (Clark 1983; Benson and Roehlekepartain 1993; Burton 1995). For example, data on child abuse, battered wives, and runaway children indicate higher rates of such disorders among two-parent families in suburban areas than among single parents in inner-city communities (Research Center on Child Abuse and Neglect 1981). Although many observers assume that two-parent families invariably function more effectively than one-parent families, many studies have found the development of children in two-parent families with stepfathers not to be much better than their development in single-parent families (McLanahan 1995).

In addition, most research studies that have assumed negative effects (such as poverty, welfare dependency, etc.) of single-parent families have often failed to distinguish whether those disadvantaged characteristics existed prior to their single-parent status. According to a recent HHS study:

> The answer provided by research to date is that pre-existing factors account for much but not all of the difficulties experienced by children and adults in single-parent families. Despite consistent evidence of greater risk, the research also shows that the majority of children in single-parent families develop normally.
> (National Center for Health Statistics 1995, xii)

Yet we do *not* assume that single-parent black families are able to function well in most family domains in every situation. In some areas, especially in the economic realm, they are at a marked disadvantage (with one earner) compared with two-parent families (with two earners). Nevertheless, many single-parent black families are able to function effectively in many domains at different stages of their life cycle because they are part of extended-family support systems.

The cultural resilience of African American families headed by women is largely based on their strong achievement orientation and work ethic. Most black single parents place major emphasis on socializing their children for higher educational and occupational attainment (Allen 1976; Clark 1983; Malson 1986; Jarrett 1994). Research studies consistently show that black female-headed families more often have positive consequences for upward mobility for themselves and their children than white female-headed families (Benson and Donahue 1989; Zill and Nord 1994).

Over the past two decades, the educational attainment of black single parents rose sharply. Between 1970 and 1990, the proportion of black women family heads with some college education soared from 8 to 26 percent, while the proportion who were high school dropouts plummeted from 66 to 29 percent. Moreover, black women who head families today have much higher educational attainment than single parents twenty years ago. Interestingly, there are about as many college-educated black women heading families as high school dropouts (Hill 1989).

The high educational attainment and aspirations of female heads of family are translated into high educational achievement of their children (Kandel 1971; Wasserman 1972; Wilson and Allen 1987; Nettles and Pleck 1994). Findings from a national survey of blacks conducted by Jerold Heiss (1975) found no empirical support for the presumed negative impact of single-parent families on black educational attainment and income. Similarly, a comprehensive study of black college students by Patricia Gurin and Edgar Epps (1975) found that family structure had no effect on the students' grades, college entrance test scores, academic performance, achievement motives, and goals. Thus, they concluded:

> The absence of the father and the family structure never influenced student motivation and aspiration. In fact, it never explained even so much as one-tenth of one percent of the variance in students' aspirations, motivation, and performance.
>     Even the question of how much parents influenced the children's educational and career goals was as much a function of family income as of intactness in the home.
> (Gurin and Epps 1975, 105-6)

Findings from the Black Pulse Survey (Hill 1981), a nationally representative survey of 3,000 black households conducted by the National Urban League Research Department in 1979-80, provide further evidence of the positive impact of families headed by black women on their children. Overall, black single-parent families (10 percent) were about as likely to have children in college as black two-parent families (13 percent).

However, when one controls for family income, single-parent families were somewhat *more* likely to have children in college than two-parent families. For example, among families with incomes between $12,000-19,999, 17 percent of the one-parent families had children in college, compared with 11 percent of the two-parent families. Similarly, among families with income under $6,000, one-parent families were three times (6 percent) more likely than two-parent families (2 percent) to have children in college.

At the same time, it is important to note that family income is an important determinant of one's ability to attend college. Black families with incomes of $20,000 and over (21 percent) are four times more likely to have a child in college than black families with incomes under $6,000 (5 percent) (Hill 1981).

An in-depth study (Freeman and Holtzer 1986) of success patterns of inner-city black males found that family structure was *not* an important factor:

> By contrast, (black) youths from homes in which both parents were present at age 14 do only marginally better than those from homes in which only one parent was present at that age, implying that, by itself, the female-headed home is not a major deterrent to socioeconomic success. (Freeman and Holtzer 1986, 374)

## BOYS REARED BY UNMARRIED MOTHERS

There is currently much debate about the ability of women to raise boys in single-parent families. Unfortunately, many advocates of the view that single mothers cannot rear boys to be men fail to realize that *no* black households--including two-parent families-- rear their children solely by themselves! Because of the unique role of the black extended family, most black families--even those in which the fathers are present--also depend on positive male and female role models who live in other households to assist in socializing their children (Jarrett 1994; Williams and Kornblum 1994). Thus, most unmarried black mothers rely on related and non-related men (as well as women) who live in other households to assist in the socialization of their male--and female--children. Joyce Aschenbrenner (1975) emphasizes this contribution of extended families:

> Most ethnographers of black communities have been men; as a result, many interpretations of Black male and female roles reflect a male bias. An instance of what I believe to be a false issue partly arising from such a bias is that of the problem of masculine identification in a matrifocal household. It should be noted that in few societies has the role of mother been undermined and generally held suspect as in middle-class, upwardly mobile America, where a strong mother is open to accusations of "Momism". . . .
>
> No particular family structure can be deemed necessary to raise children successfully, nor is any type of family a guarantee of success. A boy can learn how to exercise his rights and authority from any model, male or female. . . .The real problem in Black communities is not that of female dominance per se, but that of the single-parent household, where one adult, usually the mother, must bear the burden of socialization, even support, by herself; this may put severe strains on her relationship with her children. As we have seen in the Black family this is often mitigated by the help of grandparents, godparents, aunts, uncles, sisters, and brothers, even neighbors, in raising her children; and male members of her family, as well as the men in her life, serve as role models to her young son. (Aschenbrenner 1975, 84-85)

Useni Perkins (1993) also emphasizes the resilience of single black mothers:

> The strongest criticisms being directed at some single Black mothers is that they are unable to meet the socializing needs of Black boys and, therefore, have difficulty in raising them. . . .To be truthful, there is enough blame to spread everywhere when we clear our minds of convoluted theories, sexist biases and seriously evaluate what is happening to young Black boys. Why, then, do we place so much of this blame on single Black mothers when most of them are also victims of the same oppressive environment?. . . .Of course, many single Black mothers have difficulty raising Black boys under such conditions. But this is also true, in varying degrees, even when a father or significant other male is present.This is to say that raising Black boys today is a demanding task regardless of family composition. . . . [Nevertheless]. . . .it is reasonable to assume that most single Black mothers cannot teach Black boys all they need to know about becoming a competent and responsible man if there are no competent and responsible Black men to assist them in this task. (Perkins 1993, 2-3)

One of the black men who was reared in a single-parent family reported to Earl Hutchinson (1992):

> My uncle, aunt, sister and her husband all helped to raise me. I would spend a lot of time at their houses. They would fix food for me and take me places on the weekends. They would go to parties and I would go along with them. They encouraged me in school and they saw to it that I always had a little spending money. Even now, I still can go to them whenever I have a problem. They will help me anyway they can. (Hutchinson 1992, 30)

The reality is that thousands of black males are currently being reared by women in single-parent households. Interestingly, although the American public is ready to blame such mothers for raising the minority of males who become delinquents, criminals, and drug abusers, it is not willing to give them credit for raising the majority of males who complete high school, who graduate from college, who work every day in legitimate occupations, who are responsible fathers, and who are productive citizens of this society. Mothers cannot raise males? Tell that to the thousands of black men, such as Dr. Benjamin Carson, the famed neurosurgeon at Johns Hopkins Hospital, who dedicated his book, *Gifted Hands* (1990), " . . . to my mother, Sonya Carson, who basically sacrificed her life to make certain that my brother and I got a head start." Or, tell that to Jesse Jackson or Colin Powell, the former Chief of Staff, who were both reared in female-headed households. It is not that these women did not need men, but they sought out responsible men--and women--to assist them in raising their sons--and daughters.

## CONTACT WITH FATHERS

Interestingly, the overwhelming majority of studies of black female-headed households fail to inquire about the extent of contact that the fathers of those children have with the mothers or their children. Most researchers merely assume that if it is a family headed by a black woman, there is no need to ask about contact, because we all "know" that they have *no* contact at all.

However, the few studies that have examined the degree of non-custodial parental contact have found much higher levels than is commonly believed (Furstenberg and Nord 1985; Sullivan 1985; Furstenberg et al. 1987; Jarrett 1994; Jarrett 1995; Burton 1995). In her study of single black mothers, Harriette McAdoo (1983) found that about half of the mothers reported having contact with the fathers of their children on a regular basis. Most of them reported that their children had more contact with their fathers than they did. Furthermore, based on the National Survey of Children, Frank Furstenberg et al. (1983) found that about two out of five children in female-headed families had regular contact with their fathers. Moreover, according to conventional wisdom, men are reputed to be so obsessed by their work that they neglect their families. Yet, recent research studies clearly demonstrate that the happiness and satisfaction of fathers are more strongly related to their family roles than to their work roles (Levine and Pitt 1995). In short, most fathers want to be involved in the rearing of their children. More studies are needed that inquire about the nature and extent of contact that children in two-parent and female-headed families have with their fathers and other related males who live in the same and other households.

## UNMARRIED MALE PARENTS

One unheralded black family structure that has been increasing rapidly is the family headed by unmarried men. More and more black fathers are taking custody of their own or related children (Hutchinson 1992, 1994). Between 1970 and 1980, while families headed by men increased by 59 percent, families headed by women increased by 84 percent. However, between 1980 and 1990, black families headed by men rose twice as fast as families headed by women. In other words, 190,000 more black men headed one-parent families in 1990 (446,000) than in 1980 (256,000). Thus, between 1970 and 1990, the proportion of all black families that were headed by unmarried men rose from 4 percent to 6 percent.

The median age of these unmarried men was 42.8 years, one-third of them was under the age of 35, two-fifths were between 35-54 years old, and one-fourth were 55 years and over. Half of these men were either separated or divorced, one-fifth were widowed, and the remaining one-third were never married. Two out of five of these families headed by unmarried men were caring for children under the age of 18. Of the children in these families, three-fourths were the biological children of these unmarried men, while the remaining one-fourth were other related children, such as nieces, nephews and grandchildren. Clearly, increasing numbers of formerly-married and never married black men are assuming primary family responsibility for raising their own children or other dependent relatives (Jarrett 1994). Moreover, Burton (1995) observed that ethnographic studies have found that numerous black males, including biological and non-biological fathers, and paternal grandmothers and grandfathers play major roles in rearing related children.

Hutchinson (1992) describes a number of strategies adopted by single black fathers in raising their children. One of them reported the following:

My youngest son was six months old when he came to live with me. So I had to do the mothering as well as the fathering. I

changed his diapers, fed him, hugged and kissed him. In church,
I would sit in the section where the women with babies sat. I had
my yellow bag filled with pins, diapers, baby bottles and pacifiers.
I sat there rocking him and nursing him just like the other
mothers. I didn't care who looked or said anything. It was
something that I had to do and enjoyed doing.
(Hutchinson 1992, 28)

## ADOLESCENT DRUG ABUSE

Another example of the flexibility of black families is their
capacity to enhance resilience against drugs and other substance
abuse among low-income black youth. Although the use and abuse
of drugs is considered to be pervasive in the black community, it is
interesting how little attention is given by social scientists and the
media to the relatively low levels of substance abuse by black
adolescents (Paulin 1991; Rebach et al. 1992). National surveys of
drug use among black and white youth reveal consistently that
black youth have lower levels of usage than white youth (National
Institute on Drug Abuse 1991; Nettles and Peck 1994;
U.S. Department of Health and Human Services 1996). According
to a 1992 Health and Human Services (HHS) survey, black youth,
12-21 years old, had lower levels of substance abuse than
comparable age white youth regarding smoking cigarettes, drinking
alcohol, using marijuana, and using cocaine (National Center for
Health Statistics 1995a) (fig. 4).

An in-depth analysis (Benson and Donahue 1989) of ten-year
(1976-85) data from the Monitoring the Future surveys of high
school seniors conducted annually by the University of Michigan
revealed not only sharp declines in drug abuse among blacks
relative to whites over the ten-year period but that blacks had lower
levels of substance abuse than white youths in each category:
smoking cigarettes, drinking alcohol, and using marijuana and
cocaine.

While the extent of regular (40 times or more) alcohol use
among black boys fell sharply from 30 to 24 percent over the ten-
year period, alcohol use among white boys fell only slightly from 55
to 53 percent. Lifetime cocaine use, however, fell sharply among
black boys--from 18 to 13 percent, while it increased significantly

**Fig. 4:  Substance Abuse by Race of Youth, 1992.**

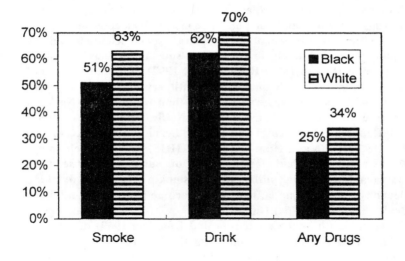

Source:              National Center for Health Statistics (1992).

among white boys--from 13 to 22 percent. Somewhat similar patterns of lower levels of abuse occurred among black and white girls. On the other hand, it is important to note that when black adolescents become adults their rates of drug use are often comparable to the rates among white adults.

Although researchers of the national surveys had obtained similar racial differences for several years, they refused to print the results because they did not believe they were credible. One of the major explanations they gave for lower substance abuse among black than white seniors was because blacks had higher dropout levels, the blacks who reached the twelfth grade was a select group of more highly-motivated youth. However, when they obtained similar racial differentials for eighth and tenth graders in 1992, the researchers had to conclude that the results among the seniors were valid:

> First, for virtually all drugs, licit and illicit, black seniors have reported lifetime and annual prevalence rates lower--sometimes dramatically lower--than those for white or Hispanic seniors. This is mostly true for the 30-day and daily prevalence statistics, as well, although there are a few exceptions.
>
> Second, the same can be said for black students in eighth and tenth grades, which means that the low usage for blacks in twelfth grade almost certainly is not due to differential dropout rates and/or a differential degree of association between dropping out and using drugs among the three racial/ethnic groups. (Johnston et al. 1993, 67)

It is also interesting to note that national surveys of drug abuse among the adult population reveal, contrary to popular belief, that substance abuse patterns among blacks are often comparable to those of whites. Of the 11.4 million Americans who were illicit drug users in 1992, whites comprised 76 percent of the users, while blacks accounted for only 14 percent--slightly higher than their 12 percent share of the total U.S. population. Moreover, the current rate of illicit drug use among black adults (6.6 percent) is only somewhat higher than the rate among white adults (5.5 percent) (National Institute on Drug Abuse 1995). Thus, while whites comprise the overwhelming majority of illicit drug abusers, blacks are highly overrepresented among persons arrested for the possession of illicit drugs (table 6).

## RESILIENT PROGRAMS

Many community-based programs designed to strengthen single-parent families have been established in inner-cities.   One exemplary effort is the Sisterhood of Black Single Mothers, founded by Daphne Busby in the Bedford-Stuyvesant section of Brooklyn, New York.   Since its inception in 1973, the program has demonstrated that the circumstances of low-income single mothers can be improved markedly by addressing their needs from an Afrocentric perspective.   By providing older single women as positive role models to young mothers, the Sisterhood has been able to enhance their sense of self-worth and to develop their skills in such areas as parenting, male-female relations, education, and employment.   This program, which started by helping single mothers to complete their high school equivalency, has motivated many to attend and graduate from college.   Many other programs targeted to young single mothers, such as the famed Pacquin High School in Baltimore, Maryland for single adolescent parents, can be found across the nation.

Numerous communities have developed programs to enhance the parenting skills of black fathers.   One of the earliest programs, launched by the National Urban League (NUL), was targeted to adolescent and young adult black men.   The NUL program sought to promote responsible sexuality, prevent out-of-wedlock pregnancies, and enhance skills to enable males to assume appropriate parental responsibility for their children.   Other innovative programs for African American fathers are the National Institute for Responsible Fatherhood and Family Revitalization founded by Charles Ballard in Cleveland, Ohio, My Child Calls Me Daddy founded by Reggie Brass in Los Angeles, California, and the Children's Network in Philadelphia, Pennsylvania.

A comprehensive study by James Levine and Edward Pitt (1995) of community strategies that enhance responsible fatherhood revealed that the most effective programs facilitate the connection of fathers to work and to their children and families.   The authors contend that a wide range of institutions (social service agencies,

TABLE 6:   ILLICIT DRUG USERS AND DRUG ARRESTS
           BY RACE, 1994

| Any Illicit Users[1] | Number[2] | Percent |
|---|---|---|
| Total | 22.7 | 100 |
| White | 17.5 | 77 |
| Black | 2.9 | 13 |
| Hispanic | 1.9 | 8 |

| Any Cocaine Users[1] | Number[2] | Percent |
|---|---|---|
| Total | 3.7 | 100 |
| White | 2.4 | 65 |
| Black | 0.7 | 19 |
| Hispanic | 0.5 | 14 |

| Any Crack Users[1] | Number[2] | Percent |
|---|---|---|
| Total | 1.3 | 100 |
| White | 0.7 | 54 |
| Black | 0.4 | 31 |
| Hispanic | 0.1 | 8 |

| Drug Arrests | Number[2] | Percent |
|---|---|---|
| Total | 1.12 | 100.0 |
| White | .68 | 60.6 |
| Black | .43 | 38.4 |

1.  Use of an illicit drug over the past year.
2.  Numbers are in millions.

*Source*:  National Institute on Drug Abuse (1995), National Household
           Survey on Drug Abuse:  1994 and U.S. Crime Report: 1994.

hospitals, schools, courts, workplace, etc.) must share the responsibility of empowering fathers in their family and work roles. Some of the exemplary programs they cite include: the Children's Aid Society Teen Primary Pregnancy Prevention Program, Planned Parenthood First Things First Male Achievement Network, Milwaukee Urban League Male Adolescent Responsibility Project, Baltimore City Healthy Start Men Services Program, Chicago's Community Renewal Society Paternal Involvement Demonstration Society, and Mad Dads, an interdenominational community-based group organized to combat crime, gangs, violence, and drug trafficking in Omaha, Nebraska. See a comprehensive listing of such programs in Levine and Pitt (1995). The National Center on Fathers and Families (NCOFF) at the University of Pennsylvania serves as a national clearinghouse for research studies that attempt to identify effective policies and programs that strengthen the family roles and involvement of fathers.

For many years, the MAAT Center, located in Washington, D.C. and founded by Dr. Aminifu R. Harvey, has implemented Afrocentric Rites of Passage programs for young males who had contact with the criminal justice system. With funds from a high-risk youth grant from the U.S. Center for Substance Abuse Prevention (CSAP), the MAAT Center instituted a Rites of Passage program between 1992 and 1995 for annual cohorts of males between the ages of 12-14 years. An in-depth evaluation conducted by the Morgan State University Institute for Urban Research found that, at the end of three years, youth who had participated in the program had more positive gains in self-esteem, racial identity, drug knowledge, and academic orientation than comparable youth who did not participate (Institute for Urban Research 1996).

# Chapter 7

## Strong Kinship Bonds

Undoubtedly, the most enduring cultural strength that black Americans brought with them from the African continent was the extended family and its strong kinship networks. Aminifu Harvey (1985) emphasizes the cultural continuity of such kinship networks:

> The deep sense of kinship has historically been one of the strongest forces in traditional African life. Kinship is the mechanism which regulates social relationships between people in a given community; almost all of the concepts pertaining to and connected with human relationships can be understood and interpreted through the kinship system.
> (Harvey 1985, 13)

Joyce Aschenbrenner identifies strong kinship bonds as one of several important cultural values in black families:

> Among these values are (1) a high value placed on children; (2) the approval of strong, protective mothers; (3) the emphasis on strict discipline and respect for elders; (4) the strength of family bonds; and (5) the ideal of the independent spirit. These values are reflected in social practices that are parallel to, but which differ significantly from, those in White communities. For example, adoption by relatives and neighbors is widely practiced in Black families. As Powdermaker and Johnson point out, Black foster parents do not try to keep their origins from foster children, nor is there a feeling that they are at a disadvantage because they are not their "real" children. This stems from the more comprehensive reach of the extended family, in which other adults besides parents take responsibility for children. Again, because relatives and friends often take in orphaned or rejected children as a matter of course, legal adoption is not as crucial in Black families as in most White families.
> (Aschenbrenner 1975, 137)

Melvin Wilson (1986) offers a useful developmental perspective to enhance understanding of the changing structures and functioning of black extended families. His framework comprises three dimensions: (a) the various life stages of extended families; (b) the antecedents and consequences of extended family life; and (c) implications for social policies and program development to enhance black family functioning.  Wilson identifies three stages of the life cycle of black extended families:

> The first stage, which is the transitional period, can involve family units that are composed of either an unattached nuclear family, a one-parent family, or a childless couple.  The second stage represents the core period of the extended family. . . .additional adult and/or child family members are absorbed into any one of the three kinds of transitional family units to form the new extended family.   The third stage, nonevolved grandparent or elderly, represents the final period of the extended family. In many instances the non-evolved elderly is the dominant figure within the extended family.  (Wilson 1986, 248)

In general the grandmother is the central figure in most black extended families  (Gillespie 1976; Furstenberg 1981; Stevens 1984; Burton 1995).  In a chapter entitled, "Granny: The Guardian of the Generations," E. Franklin Frazier (1948) described the unique contributions of grandmothers to black extended families:

> The energy, courage, and devotion of this woman, who was nearly seventy, are characteristic of the role which the grandmother has played in the Negro family.  During slavery the Negro grandmother occupied in many instances an important place in the plantation economy and was highly esteemed by both the slaves and the masters. . . .
>     The grandmother's prestige and importance were as great among the slaves on the plantation as among the whites in the master's house.  She was the repository of the accumulated lore and superstition of the slaves and was on hand at the birth of black children as well as of white.  She took under her care the orphaned and abandoned children. . .
>     When emancipation came, it was often the old grandmother who kept the generations together. . . .Thus, it has been the grandmother who has held the generations together when fathers and even mothers abandoned their off-spring.  (Frazier 1948, 114-17)

According to conventional wisdom, the black extended family is reputed to have declined and is claimed to be virtually nonexistent today in most urban areas.  However, research studies reveal that the proportion of black extended families continued to rise over the past two decades.  Between 1970 and 1980, the proportion of black extended family households increased from 23 to 28 percent (Farley and Allen 1987), and by 1992, according to the National Survey of Family Households, one out of three (34 percent) black households were three-generational. Unfortunately, the declining availability of affordable housing has contributed to thousands of low-income families having to "double-up" with relatives in multigenerational households.

## SERVICES TO UNWED MOTHERS

One of the most important services provided by black kinship networks is support to single mothers, especially teen mothers. Nine out of ten babies born to black teenagers live with their mother in the homes of their grandparents or other relatives. Thus, if there has been an epidemic of adolescent pregnancies in the black community, there has also been an epidemic of three-generational families. Many studies (Furstenberg 1981; Malson 1986; Sandven and Resnick 1990; Jayakody et al. 1993; Berrick and Barth 1994; Jarrett 1995; Burton et al. 1995) have revealed that kin provide a wide range of support to young single mothers, often enabling them to complete their education or to obtain a job.

However, many extended families today differ markedly from those generations ago in that many of the present-day grandmothers are between the ages of 30 and 40 years old, while many of them were between the ages of 45 to 55 years old in the past. Although the three-generational structure continues to exist, its viability has diminished because grandmothers are less available as child care providers. Moreover, as Burton (1995) reminds us, the decline in employment opportunities and other economic resources in black communities has made it more difficult for many kinship networks to provide support to their relatives today than was possible in past decades. Clearly, multigenerational black households need additional support from both the private and public sectors.

## DAY-CARE SERVICES

African American kinship networks nevertheless continue to provide short-term child-care services, especially to working parents. Two-fifths of working black mothers depend on responsible relatives for day-care services at moderate costs, and the bulk of those services are provided by grandmothers. Such affordable day -care services by kin permit thousands of parents to hold important jobs in order to maintain the economic stability of their families (Malson 1983; Jayakody et al. 1993; Jarrett 1995). During the 1970s, federal income tax regulations penalized families who relied on kin for day care by allowing child-care deductions only for children who were cared for by nonrelatives. Fortunately, such anti-family policies have been changed to permit tax deductions for children cared for by relatives.

## INFORMAL ADOPTION

The informal adoption or the rearing of children or caring for adults by members of their extended family for short or long periods of time is still very pervasive in the African American community (Hill 1977; Stack 1974; Martin and Martin 1978; Sandven and Resnick 1990). Over the past two decades, the number of informally adopted children living with relatives has risen sharply among black families. Between 1970 and 1990, the number of black children living in extended-family households rose from 1.3 million to 1.6 million, raising the proportion of informally adopted children from 13 to 16 percent (U.S. Bureau of the Census 1992).

Of the 1.6 informally adopted black children, 52 percent live with only their mothers, 3 percent with only their fathers, and 4 percent with both parents in the homes of relatives. However, the remaining 41 percent live in the homes of relatives without either parent present. Three-fourths of these informally adopted children are being reared by grandparents, while the remaining one-fourth are being reared by aunts, uncles, or other relatives. Moreover, single-parent black families are three times more likely to informally adopt children than two-parent black families.

## FOSTER CARE

Despite the fact that thousands of black families provide extensive informal adoption and informal foster-care services, many child welfare agencies have not targeted, until recently, kinship networks for such services. Of the one million black children currently living in the households of relatives without either parent, 80 percent are informally adopted by kin, while the remaining 20 percent are in foster care. While child welfare agencies find it difficult to obtain permanent homes for 200,000 black children in foster care, the black extended family has succeeded in finding homes for 800,000 black children. According to the NUL Black Pulse Survey, a nationally representative survey of blacks, 40 percent (or 3,600,000) of the respondents were interested in taking in a foster child.

This would translate into about twelve black families for each of the 200,000 black children in foster care. The black extended family should be viewed as a major resource for foster care and adoptive placements.

As a result of the increasing unavailability of nonrelatives for traditional foster care placement, there has been a recent surge in the number of children who are placed with relatives. The sharp increase in children placed with kin has resulted in the creation of a new foster-care category called *kinship care* (Berrick and Barth 1994; Wilson and Chipungu 1996). In some cities, such as New York and Baltimore, the majority of children in foster care are placed with relatives.

Unfortunately, many of the kinship care families are being used as "dumping grounds." The low-income aunts or grandmothers who care for their kin receive the lower AFDC grant for child care and are denied or discouraged from obtaining the higher foster-care stipends. In addition, many of the kinship care families are not provided important social services. Such lack of social support increases the social stress, economic hardships, and excessive burdens for these grandmothers, because many of the children in kinship care have more severe health needs than other foster care placements, especially those who were born to alcohol-addicted, drug-addicted, or HIV-infected mothers (Burton 1992). Research reveals that children in kinship care families have more stable placements than children in nonrelative foster care (Le Prohn 1994; Wilson and Chipungu 1996). Thus, kinship families should be viewed by public and private agencies as vital foster care resources for quality, long-term placements for children who are not able to return to their biological parents (Burton 1996).

On reaching the age of emancipation, many black children often leave the foster-care system to live in the homes of kin (Westat 1992). Clearly, those kin should have been given greater consideration for foster care placements when the children first entered the system. We are pleased with the section of Title V of the Personal Responsibility and Work Opportunity Reconciliation Act of 1996 that permits states to give priority to relatives for foster care and adoptive placements. We only hope that states also provide adequate social and economic resources to those kinship care families.

## FORMAL ADOPTION

Most traditional agencies place priority for adoption on families that are: two parents, middle income, have no children, and are relatively young. Such practices structurally discriminate against and screen out thousands of families of color that are: single parents, low income, with dependent children, and are middle-aged. Furthermore, many families that respond to appeals for adoption are turned off or discouraged by culturally insensitive homestudies, complex regulations, and protracted procedures.

There have been numerous instances in which hundreds of interested blacks responded to adoption campaigns, but only a fraction of the families had an adopted children placed with them. During the 1980s, for example, the Urban League participated in an adoption campaign that recruited over eight hundred black families, but only two of the families were able to have children placed with them (McRoy et al. 1997). Recruiting enough black families is not a major problem but retaining them is. To enhance retention, specialized minority adoption agencies, such as the Institute for Black Parenting headed by Zena Ogelsby, have instituted "rapid-response" procedures that maintain regular contract with families that have been recruited, while incorporating culturally sensitive practices (McRoy et al. 1997).

Although black families informally adopt children to a greater extent than white families, national data also reveal that African American families formally adopt children to the same extent as, and sometimes more than, white families (Mason and Williams 1985). An analysis by the U.S. Children's Bureau (1984) found that black couples adopted at a higher rate than white couples. According to the 1987 National Health Interview Survey (NCHS 1990), the proportion of women 20-44 years of age who had formally adopted children was about the same among blacks (1.5 percent) and whites (1.8 percent).

Such data refute the conventional justification for transracial adoption of black children: there are not enough black families who are interested in legally adopting children. Actually, the national campaigns to encourage transracial adoption are misleading, since their primary interest is in obtaining healthy black infants, not the older, waiting children. The section of Title V of the 1996 Personal Responsibility and Work Opportunity Reconciliation Act that discourages same-race adoption placements is misguided because it will not markedly reduce the number of waiting children. It will only permit private agencies to make more healthy black infants available to interested white parents for fees over $20,000. The older black children in foster care will continue to wait long periods for permanent homes.

Such insensitive policies fail to build on the successful efforts of culturally sensitive adoption agencies that demonstrate it is possible to recruit and retain enough black families who want to adopt black children. According to the NUL Black Pulse Survey, one out of three (or 3,000,000) of the families said they were interested in formally adopting black children. Thus, there were about 100 black families available for each of the approximately 30,000 black foster children who were freed for adoption (Hill et al. 1993).

These findings support the long-standing positions of such groups as the National Association of Black Social Workers about: (a) the availability of sufficient black homes for black children; and (b) the cultural insensitivity and inadequacy of home studies, training, recruitment, and retention efforts in the black community by many traditional adoption agencies.  On the other hand, many specialized minority adoption agencies, such as the Institute for Black Parenting, Homes for Black Children, Spaulding for Children, National Association of Black Social Workers, etc., have little trouble finding black families for waiting black children. Clearly, culturally sensitive and competent strategies are needed to recruit, and retain, the thousands of black families who are genuinely interested in formally adopting black children (McPhatter 1997).

## FICTIVE KIN

It is important to observe that the African American extended family extends beyond blood relatives, and includes "fictive kin," that is, unrelated individuals who often provide more family support services than blood kin. Many informally adoptive children, for example, were reared by surrogate parents who were not their biological grandparents, or aunts, or uncles (Martin and Martin 1987; Jarrett 1995; Manns 1988).  Furthermore, many persons selected as godparents are often nonrelatives who were very close to the family.  Since godparents agree to assume primary responsibility for rearing their god children if their parents are unable to do so, foster care and adoption agencies should give them priority for the placement of children, even if they are not blood kin.

In her in-depth study of the importance of "significant others" in contributing to the stability and advancement of black individuals and families, Wilhelmina Manns (1988) found that 64 percent of the persons who were cited as influential "significant others" were nonrelatives:

> Most of the family friend (close nonkin) significant others performed supplemental parenting roles--nurturing--through the mode of emotional

support. A middle-class female, though loved by her two busy and task-oriented parents, remembered a close family friend who was uneducated but who saw me as a child always. She was one of those very good people who always give tender, loving care. She had the capacity to give and the capacity to love. She nurtured me; my mother did not. She gave me something to fall back on; somebody who was always there. (Manns 1988, 281)

We also include foster parents who have bonded with children over long periods of time as part of the child's extended family. Fortunately, increasing numbers of progressive agencies are permitting foster parents to be adoptive parents to children who have been languishing in foster care. We recommend that foster care and adoption regulations should be modified to include a broader range of blood relatives (especially cousins) and nonrelatives (godparents, foster parents, and other fictive kin) as part of the "kinship" network for foster care or adoptive placements.

## REDUCING CHILD ABUSE

The extended family has been a major contributor to the relatively low levels of child abuse in black families (Giovannoni and Billingsley 1970; Hill 1977). Andrew Billingsley (1973) observed:

It is not generally appreciated, for example, that child neglect and abuse are much more common in white families than in black families. Child neglect is much more common among lower-class white families than among lower-class black families. Child abuse is much more likely to occur in white families than in black families who live in similar, or even worse, economic circumstances. (Billingsley 1973, 314)

Although black families are over represented in the official reported statistics on child abuse and neglect, national surveys have consistently revealed relatively low incidences of child abuse among blacks (Garbarino and Ebata 1983). The National Incidence Survey conducted for the U.S. National Center on Child Abuse and Neglect in 1979-80 found:

In general, incidence rates seem to be about the same for white and nonwhite children. For white children, incidence rates for all forms of maltreatment were much higher in low-income groups than in the higher income groups. For non-white children, incidence rates for neglect were higher in low-income groups and incidence rates for abuse were <u>low</u> and constant across income levels. (Resource Center for Child Abuse 1981: 2)

The National Incidence Surveys of 1986 and 1993 also obtained similar findings about the lack of significant racial difference in abuse and neglect as the first NIS. Thus, Sedlack and Broadhurst (1996) concluded:

> The NIS-3 found <u>no</u> race difference in maltreatment incidence. The NIS-3 reiterates the findings on the earlier national incidence studies in this regard. That is, the NIS-1 and NIS-2 also found <u>no significant race differences</u> in the incidence of maltreatment or maltreatment-related injuries.
>
> Service providers may find these results somewhat surprising in view of the disproportionate representation of children of color in the child welfare population and in the clinetele of other public agencies. However, it should be recognized that the NIS methodology identifies a much broader range of children than those who come to the attention of any one type of service agency or the even smaller subset who receive child protective and other child welfare services. The NIS finding suggest that the different races receive differential attention somewhere during the process of referral, investigation, and service allocation, and the differential representation of minorities in the child welfare population does not derive from inherent differences in the rates at which they are abused or neglected. (Sedlack and Broadhurst 1996)

Social scientists (Cazenave and Straus 1979; Korbin 1981) have found a direct correlation between child abuse and the proximity of relatives among blacks:

> For black parents, there is a definite difference in child abuse between those who do and those who do not have relatives living nearby. The highest rates of child abuse occur among black parents whose husbands have no relatives (35%) or wives who have no relatives (20%) living within one hour away. This type of social isolation appears to have adverse consequences for these black respondents.
> (Cazenave and Straus 1979, 292)

The close proximity and frequent contact of extended family members are major reasons why child abuse is relatively low among most black families. Not surprisingly, the lowest levels of child abuse are found among children who live in informally adoptive families (Hill 1977; 1981). On the other hand, children whose parents are socially isolated from kin are at much greater risk of experiencing child abuse. In addition, the recent surge of crack cocaine in inner cities has also contributed to higher levels of child abuse and neglect in black families.

## MUTUAL AID

Many social scientists (Jeffers 1967; TenHouton 1970; Hayes and Mindel 1973; Stack 1974, 1996; Martineau 1977; Taylor 1985; Wilson 1986; Seltzer and Bianchi 1988; Tolson and Wilson 1990) have found the mutual aid network of black extended families to be a major source of economic stability for many low-income families. Carol Stack (1974) underscores the importance of these networks:

> Few if any black families living on welfare for the second generation are able to accumulate a surplus of the basic necessities to be able to remove themselves from poverty or from the collective demands of Kin. Without the help of Kin, fluctuations in the meager flow of available goods could easily destroy a family's ability to survive. . . .Despite the relatively high cost of rent and food in urban black communities, the collective power within kin-based exchange network keeps people from going hungry. (Stack 1974, 33)

A major reason why extended family networks continue to have such strong impact on black households is the close proximity of kin. Although it is commonly believed that most people live far distances from relatives, 85 percent of the respondents in the NUL Black Pulse Survey reported they had one or more relatives who lived outside their households, but in the same city (Hill 1981). When they were asked where more than half of their relatives live, 53 percent of the respondents in the National Survey of Black Americans said that over half of their kin lived within the same city. Moreover, 38 percent of the NSBA respondents said that they had contact with their relatives daily, while 28 percent had contact with kin at least once a week (Hatchett et al. 1991). Furthermore, ethnographic studies have found that black single parents often enhance mobility for their children by sending them to schools in "better" neighborhoods where kin reside (Jarrett, 1994; Burton 1995).

According to the NUL Black Pulse Survey, lending or borrowing money was the most frequent form of mutual aid between relatives, and the provision of child care or transportation assistance was the second most frequent type of support between kin. Thirty-three percent of all black household heads reported that over the past two years, they had lent money to kin; 27 percent gave child-care services; and 26 percent provided transportation aid to relatives. On the other hand, 23 percent borrowed money from relatives; 21 percent received transportation aid; and 17 percent received child-care support from relatives. Clearly, "What goes 'round comes 'round."

Another form of frequent contact between relatives is family reunions. About half (46 percent) of the Black Pulse Survey respondents said that they hold family reunions on a regular basis (that is, every year or every two years). Middle-income blacks were more likely to have family reunions than low-income blacks. Six out of ten (63 percent) households with incomes of $20,000 or more held family reunions, compared with four out of ten (38 percent) blacks with incomes under $6,000. Many low-income families attend reunions less often than middle-income families because of the additional economic resources that are needed to participate in regular family reunions.

## RESILIENT PROGRAMS

Many community-based groups provide innovative adoption and family preservation services that reinforce kinship networks. One of the oldest groups is Home for Black Children (HBC) founded by Sydney Duncan in Detroit, Michigan during the late 1960s. Alarmed by the large number of black children who were available for adoption but were languishing in foster care, HBC was determined to demonstrate that there are more than enough families in the African American community willing and able to provide wholesome environments for children who need homes. Over a ten-year period, HBC succeeded in finding adoptive homes for over 700 black children. HBC now places greater emphasis on family preservation to prevent unnecessary foster care placements.

Other innovative adoption agencies that are able to find black homes for black foster children include: Institute for Black Parenting founded by Zena Ogelsby (Inglewood, California); Roots, Inc. founded by Toni Oliver; Akiba (Akron, Ohio); Black Family Outreach (Little Rock, Arkansas); Harlem-Dowling Children's Service (New York City); Medina Children's Service (Seattle, Washington); National Association of Black Social Workers (New York City); and Spaulding for Children (Michigan, Kansas, New

York, and Ohio).  An example of an innovative adoption project is Bandele, which is operated by a coalition of five churches under the administration of Spaulding for Children to recruit adoptive homes for special needs black boys in Michigan.  In addition to recruiting and training potentially adoptive parents, Bandele also provides cultural sensitivity training to foster care and adoption workers in public and private agencies.  Unlike most adoption programs, Bandele also provides support to surrogate parents, such as kinship parents, stepparents and informally adoptive parents.

Some of the most effective family support groups in inner cities have reinforced existing extended-family networks or developed surrogate extended families where none existed previously.  One pervasive program is mentoring, which encourages adults to serve as positive role models, as Big Brothers or Big Sisters, to at-risk youth.  Such services provide extended family functions.  A comprehensive nationwide study (Tierney et al. 1995) conducted by Public Private Ventures (PPV) found that youth who had Big Brothers and Big Sisters had lower rates of alcohol and drug use, school absences, and poor grades than control youth with no mentors.  Similarly, the House of Umoja, founded by Sister Falaka Fattah, successfully used the African extended-family model to reduce gang violence and delinquency among troubled black youth in Philadelphia.  Umjoa channeled the energies of former gang members into productive endeavors, such as helping to build Urban Boys Town, a comprehensive community-based residential center for troubled youth, and creating a variety of youth-operated businesses (Woodson 1981).

There needs to be an expansion of Afrocentric youth programs that use the extended-family concept to enhance the development of African American youth.  Examples of such programs include: SIMBA, a Rites of Passage Program for boys, directed by Paul Hill at the East End Neighborhood House in Cleveland, Ohio; the Institute of Positive Education in Chicago, Illinois; the HAWK Federation in Oakland, California; African American Men's Leadership Council's Males Rites of Passage Program in Baltimore, Maryland; and the Louis Armstrong Manhood Development Program in New Orleans, Louisiana.

# Chapter 8

# Strong Religious Orientation

There is widespread agreement that African cultural continuities in religious beliefs and behavior exist among black Americans (Mbiti 1970; Wimberly 1979; Swan 1981; Harvey 1985; Sernett 1985). According to W. E. B. Du Bois (1903, 213): "The Negro church of today is the social centre of Negro life in the United States and the most characteristic expressions of African character." Herskovits (1941) devoted an entire chapter to summarizing research related to "Africanisms in Religious Life."

Black American religious expressions identified by Melville Herskovits (1941) as African residuals include the hypnotic influence of the minister, the nature of sermons, belief in the supernatural, audience participation, hand-clapping, food-tapping, the rhythm of songs, spirituals, dance, shouting, possession by spirits, body movements during possession, baptism by total immersion, voodooism, revivals, faith healing, and funeral rituals. Aminifu Harvey (1985) also identified African vestiges in black Christian churches in the role of the minister, rituals of holy communion, the symbol of the cross, the symbol of the snake, the black ministerial robe, the call and response, the singing of spirituals, shouting, and possession by the spirit.

The Black Church was responsible for developing the first self-help societies in the black community. In 1787, two freed blacks in Philadelphia, Richard Allen and Absalom Jones, founded the Free African Society. Allen went on to establish Mother Bethel of the African Methodist Episcopal Church in 1794, and Absalom Jones organized the African Protestant Episcopal Church of St. Thomas. A similar development occurred in New York when black churchmen of the John Street Methodist Episcopal Church sought to hold "meetings of their own." Chief among these Methodists were Abraham Thompson, June Scott, Francis Jacobs, Peter Williams, and James Varick. They organized an African Chapel in 1796 that led to the formation of the A.M.E. Zion Church ("Mother Zion") in 1801. Some of the other early black churches established by free blacks were the Harrison Street Baptist Church in Petersburg, Virginia (1776); Negro Baptist Church in Williamsburg, Virginia (1785); First African Baptist Church in Savannah, Georgia (1785); Springfield Baptist Church in Augusta, Georgia (1787); Joy Street African Baptist Church in Boston (1805); Abyssinian Baptist Church in New York (1808); and First African Baptist Church in Philadelphia (1809) (Woodson 1972, 61-77).

The early black churches created numerous institutions, such as banks, insurance companies, credit unions, hospitals, orphanages, low-income housing, and homes for the elderly. The Black Church also placed a major emphasis on education by forming schools for free blacks as well as for slaves. Numerous slaves were taught by religious educators in their slave quarters. Most Sabbath Schools provided the basis for creating elementary and normal schools for free blacks.

Black churches were also responsible for establishing colleges for black youth. Some of the colleges created by the A.M.E. Church include Wilberforce (Wilberforce, Ohio, 1856), Morris Brown (Atlanta, Georgia, 1881), Allen (Columbia, South Carolina, 1870); Paul Quinn (Waco, Texas, 1881), Shorter Junior College (North Little Rock, Arkansas, 1886) and Edward Waters (Jacksonville, Florida, 1901). Similarly, some of the colleges created by the United Methodists (or Methodist Episcopal) include: Bennett College, Bethune-Cookman, Clark University, Dillard University, Meharry Medical School, and Morgan State University.

## RELIGIOUS COMMITMENT

One of the most pervasive cultural strengths of African Americans is their strong religious commitment. Studies reveal that religion tends to play a greater role in the lives of blacks than whites. According to a 1994 Gallup poll, 82 percent of black adults said that religion was "very important" in their lives, compared to only 55 percent of white adults (Gallup 1995). Similarly, national surveys consistently reveal that black youth are twice as likely as white youth to feel that religion was "very important" in their lives (U.S. Department of Health and Human Services 1996). The overwhelming majority of blacks belong to churches and attend them regularly. Based on the National Urban League Black Pulse Survey, three-fourths of all blacks belong to churches, and two-thirds attend them at least once a month. Seventy-one percent of all black parents send their children to Sunday School regularly.

An analysis of data from the National Survey of Black Americans (NSBA) by Robert Taylor and Linda Chatters (1991) revealed that overwhelming majorities of blacks participated in various religious activities several times a month or more frequently: praying (93 percent), watching or listening to religious programs (82 percent), and reading religious material (74 percent).  Eighty-three percent of the respondents felt that the Black Church had helped black people to improve their conditions, and 64 percent said that they had received some support from churches and their members (Taylor and Chatters 1991).  According to a study by the Joint Center for Political and Economic Studies, over two-thirds of the monies that blacks contribute to charity go to churches (Carson 1987).

Researchers who include religion as a variable in their studies have found it to be an important explanatory factor of positive outcomes, especially among blacks (Taylor and Chatters 1991; Jarrett 1995).  An in-depth analysis (Freeman and Holtzer 1986) found that church attendance was the most important factor for helping young black males to "escape" from inner-city poverty and to achieve positive outcomes (such as regular school attendance, productive work, and positive social activities).  An analysis (Benson and Donahue 1989) of data from the Monitoring the Future Surveys of drug abuse among high school seniors found that strong religious attitudes (that is, the degree of importance they attach to religion) was a major determinant of lower levels of substance abuse among black and white youths.

## THE COMPENSATORY THESIS

According to the compensatory thesis, blacks are said to have higher levels of religiosity than whites in order to compensate for lower social and economic status relative to whites.  Low-income blacks are expected to have higher levels of religious participation than middle-income blacks.  However, findings from several national surveys refute this explanation.  According to the NUL Black Pulse Survey, middle-income blacks were somewhat more likely than low-income blacks to belong to church (75 percent to 71 percent), and to attend church each week (48 percent to 44 percent), although neither difference was statistically significant.  Similarly, the NSBA survey also failed to find statistically significant differences between income groups related to church membership or church attendance.  Moreover, contrary to the compensatory thesis, the NSBA survey found the levels of religious participation to be higher among college-educated than noncolleged blacks, and among married than formerly-married or never-married blacks (Taylor 1988).

## CONTEMPORARY ROLE OF THE BLACK CHURCH

What is the contemporary role of the Black Church, and what types of services do they provide to strengthen black families and communities? Which churches and ministers are more likely than other churches and ministers to provide outreach programs?  C. Eric Lincoln and Lawrence Mamiya (1990) contend that many analyses of the Black Church tend to be static; they often classify churches into specific types, such as "other-wordly," "this-wordly," "isolated," "socially active," etc.  In order to properly understand the complexity of the Black Church in an historical perspective, these scholars offer a dialectical model that describes these institutions as continually experiencing tensions from polar opposites that usually shift over time.  The Lincoln and Mamiya model posits a set of six dialetically-related polar tensions:

(1) *Priestly and Prophetic*: Priestly functions involve internal activities, such as worship and maintaining the spiritual life of members, while prophetic functions refer to involvement in secular matters, such as community uplift, and politics.

(2)  *Other-Wordly and This-Wordly*: An other-wordly orientation is concerned with heaven, eternal life, and after death, while a this-wordly orientation is concerned with improving social and economic conditions in the here and now.

(3) *Universalism and Paternalism*: Universalism refers to the orientation of churches that emphasizes the universalism or "color-blindness" of the gospel rather than focus on the particularism of addressing past and current racism.

(4)  *Privatistic and Communal*: A privatistic orientation refers to churches (and ministers) who believe that their mission is to focus on the religious needs of their members, while a communal orientation refers to churches (and ministers) that believe their mission is to address the social and economic needs of their members and the surrounding communities.

(5) *Bureaucratic and Charismatic*: Bureaucratic refers to churches (and ministers) who are responsive to bureaucratic authority or hierarchy, while charismatic refers to churches (and ministers) that exercise much autonomy and flexibility.

(6)  *Accommodation and Resistance*: Accommodation refers to orientation of churches (and ministers) who view their role as mediators or cultural brokers between the races, while resistance refers to churches (and ministers) who are prepared to confront white officials or institutions, when

necessary, and are not afraid to affirm their African American cultural heritage.

In order to obtain systematic data on the characteristics and functions of black churches, Lincoln and Mamiya undertook a nationwide study in 1979 of 2,150 black congregations and 1,894 ministers from the seven major black denominations. The church sample comprised 619 rural and 1,531 urban congregations, and the minister sample comprised 363 rural and 1,531 urban clergy. Their study emphasized the diversity of black churches. About half of the churches were Baptists, one-third were Methodists, and about 15 percent were Pentacostals and other affiliations.

The median size of the black churches in the sample was 200 members-- half were above 200, and half were below. Two out of ten had 600 or more members, while three out of ten had less than 100 members. About two-thirds of the churches reported that they had cooperated with social agencies in addressing community problems. The median age of the clergy was 51.5 years, and two-thirds of the ministers were college-educated. Over half of the clergy were full-time ministers and had no other jobs. Only three percent of the clergy were women.

In order to obtain more in-depth data on the type and extent of community outreach programs in black churches, Andrew Billingsley (1994) conducted telephone surveys of 630 congregations representing twenty denominations in a dozen states of the North and Midwest in 1990-91. Subsequent surveys of black churches were conducted in metropolitan areas of Denver, Colorado, and Atlanta, Georgia, during 1992-94.

Many of the characteristics of churches were similar in the Billingsley and Lincoln-Mamiya studies. In the Billingsley study, the median size of the black churches was 175 members. Forty-four percent were Baptists, 26 percent were Methodists, and 13 percent had other affiliations. The median age of the ministers was 52 years, and 65 percent were college-educated. However, there was a higher proportion of female ministers in the Billingsley study (7 percent) than in the Lincoln-Mamiya study (3 percent).

In order to examine the relative emphasis that ministers place on their privatistic and communal functions, the Billingsley study (1994) asked whether they saw the primary role of their churches to be: (a) serving their members only; (b) serving their community; or (c) both. Eighty-six percent of the ministers believed that their mission was to address both constituents; eight percent felt that their primary mission was to address the needs of the community; and only five percent felt that their primary mission was to address the needs of their members. Similar to Lincoln-Mamiya, the

Billingsley study found that two-thirds (67 percent) of the churches had community outreach programs.

What factors were strongly correlated with having outreach programs? Churches that were more likely to have outreach programs were large, old, had more financial resources, and had college-educated and/or seminary-trained ministers. Yet, it should be clearly stated that large numbers of churches that were small and medium-sized, moderate age, with modest financial resources and with ministers with less than a college education, also had outreach programs. The outreach programs of black churches reflected ministries that fell into four areas: needy adult individuals and family support (51 percent), children and youth (31 percent), community and economic development (10 percent), and elderly (8 percent) **(fig. 5)**.

## COMMUNITY OUTREACH FUNCTIONS OF THE CHURCH

However, as Lincoln and Mamiya observe, several issues will continue to face black churches during the twenty-first century: (a) its increasing community outreach functions; (b) increasing class polarity; (c) the status of women; and (d) the underrepresentation of men.

Historically, the Black Church has been a major contributor to upward mobility for many low-income black families because of its family support functions (Billingsley 1992; Billingsley 1994; Brashears and Roberts 1995; Jarrett 1995). Yet, the declining federal role in assisting poor children and adults will clearly translate into an expanded social welfare role for black churches during the 21st century. Churches will be expected to continue to provide food, shelter, clothing, and counseling to thousands of poor single-parent families, the homeless, the infirm, the unemployed, and the incarcerated. However, faith-based institutions will have to confront new problems, such as assisting persons with HIV/AIDS, helping children of parents who are alcohol-addicted, drug-addicted and AIDS-infected, and providing drug treatment and prevention services and programs to inner-city residents. Unfortunately, many of these religious institutions will have to provide expanded social welfare services with reduced government resources.

The community and economic development functions of the Black Church will also increase markedly during the 21st century. While the social welfare functions of the black churches have been frequently noted, their economic functions have not been often acknowledged:

**Fig. 5: Type of Church Outreach Programs**

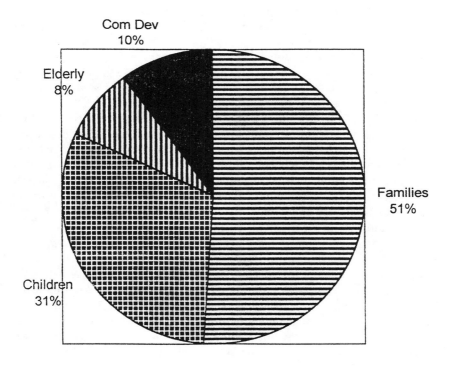

Source: Billingsley (1994).

> Black churches have not only been the spawning ground for a variety of economic enterprises such as funeral homes, benevolent associations, banks, and insurance companies, but they are themselves significant economic and financial institutions. (Lincoln and Mamiya 1990, 253)

The average annual income of the churches in the Lincoln/ Mamiya study ranged between $15,000-$24,999. Their primary means of raising monies were: offerings (85 percent), pledges (55 percent), special fund-raising drives (46 percent), and other avenues (such as church dinners, etc.). While 16 percent of the churches said that they had income from investments, 14 percent said that they owned income-producing property. Seven percent of them said that they owned some businesses, such as bookstores, parking lots, schools, child-care centers, etc. Over half of the churches have paid employees other than the ministers. In short, not only have many churches established businesses, many of them also operate as business enterprises.

One-fifth of the churches in the Billingsley study reported that they were involved in community and economic development activities, often through community development corporations to enhance the social and economic conditions of their communities. While their major community development activities focused on building housing for low-income people and the elderly, their economic development activities included credit unions, cooperatives, and small businesses. In fact, 8 percent of the churches said they operated small businesses (Hill 1994).

With the devolution of federal programs to the states through such mechanisms as block grants, states will be turning increasingly to the nonprofit sector, especially churches, to take on larger roles to enhance the community and economic development of inner-city communities. Consequently, many black churches are forming collaboratives or alliances with churches from various denominations in order to discharge this larger role more effectively. Thus, the economic functions of the church in inner-city communities are likely to expand markedly in the coming decades.

## INCREASING CLASS POLARITY

A major issue that many black churches face is the increasing polarity between the class status of their members and the class status of residents in the surrounding community. As many church members achieve upward mobility, they often move away from the low-income communities where their churches are located to middle-income communities in other parts of the city or in the suburbs.  It becomes increasingly difficult for those church members to identify with the issues and concerns of the members and non-members who still reside in the community.   Thus, tensions and disagreements often develop as residents perceive churches, most of whose members do not live in the community, as not being responsive to local concerns.  Black churches need to increase their sensitivity to the concerns of the community by establishing stronger collaboration with the residents.

## THE STATUS OF WOMEN

The status of women in black churches will be another issue of increasing importance in coming decades. Although women have historically outnumbered men as church members, they continue to occupy subordinate roles as church leaders.  While females accounted for about 70 percent of the church members in the Lincoln-Mamiya study, they comprised only three percent of the ministers.   Moreover, although women are over-represented among the leadership of most church auxiliaries, such as ushers associations, missionaries, Sunday Schools, youth groups, choirs, etc., they continue to be underrepresented on policy-making groups, such as trustees, etc.  Fortunately, increasing numbers of churches are appointing women to leadership positions on policy-making boards, as assistant ministers, and as senior pastors.   Clearly, sexism in the Black Church must be more effectively combatted in the twenty-first century.

## THE UNDERREPRESENTATION OF MEN

The underrepresentation of male youth and adults as members has been a historic problem for most black churches.  While males comprised only 26 percent of all adults in the Lincoln-Mamiya study, males accounted for only 29 percent of all the youth.  Thus, males account for about three out of ten church members, wherefore, the perennial lament, "Where are the black men?" or "Why don't more black men attend church?" In order to obtain answers to these questions, Jawanza Kunjufu (1994) conducted field observations, formal interviews, and developed a questionnaire that was administered to black males.  He held an overnight retreat, which was attended by 75 men, to discuss their reasons for not attending church. Kunjufu identified twenty-one reasons, which we have classified into five groups: (a) characteristics of the minister; (b) characteristics of the church;

(c) characteristics of the sermons; (d) characteristics of the members; and (e) other reasons.

Many males reported they did not attend church because the ministers were too hypocritical (they said one thing and did another) and too dictatorial (they were too egotistical and overbearing). The characteristics of the church that offended them were an overemphasis on class status, money, tithing, and proper dress. Most of the men were turned off by the sermons, which they felt were too emotional, long, irrelevant, Eurocentric, and overemphasized passivity, faith, Heaven, and condemnation of various types of behavior (dancing, smoking, drinking, sex, etc.). Some of the men said they did not attend church because its membership did not have enough male role models and had too many homosexuals. Other reasons for not attending included: illiteracy (they could not read the Bible, hymnals, etc.); their parents' double standards (mothers encouraged daughters but not sons to attend); bonding with non-attending peer groups; competing priorities; and they did not need to attend church because of individual spirituality.

Kunjufu (1994) examined each of the reasons and discussed their strengths and weaknesses, while exposing some of them as rationalizations. Nevertheless, he contends that black churches will only attract black men when they assign high priority to developing ministries that address issues about which men are concerned. An examination of churches that are successful in attracting men seems to strongly support Kunjufu's assertions. Why has the Nation of Islam been able to recruit and retain a strong representation of males in its membership? Men have clearly defined roles in the Nation of Islam and occupy many positions of authority. Unfortunately, Muslim women do not often hold equal positions of authority. Yet, many Christian churches are also successful in attracting male members, notably Pentacostals, Holiness, Apostolic, United Church of Christ, Church of God in Christ, Adventists, as well as many Baptist, Methodist, and Catholic congregations. The churches that are most successful in attracting black males, according to Kunjufu, are "liberation" churches:

> Liberation churches have a male population which exceeds 25 to 30 percent, have ministries for males, and have study sessions where these twenty-one reasons and more have been discussed. . . .
> I pray that those pastors of entertainment and containment churches will pray for a vision to design ministries that will be attractive to African American men. (Kunjufu 1994, 115)

Churches that succeed in attracting black men go beyond Men's Day programs, and have other activities: Men's Week, Men's Retreats, Men's Fellowship/Support Groups, Bible Study, Afrocentric Reading Groups, Mentoring for Boys, Rites of Passage, and Community of Men (groups of men who engage in community-wide activities to reduce crime, violence and drugs) (Kunjufu 1994).

## RESILIENT PROGRAMS

We will now provide a brief overview of promising initiatives by black congregations that are designed to strengthen children, youth, families, and black communities. Billingsley (1992, 1994) and Lincoln and Mamiya (1990) provide case studies of many innovative outreach programs by a broad cross-section of black churches. To increase their assistance to inner-city families, increasing numbers of black churches have set up Quality of Life Centers to address the broad range of needs of all family members. Services provided by such centers include day care, pre-school programs, nurseries, parenting education, family counseling, remedial education, family planning, substance abuse prevention, employment training, recreational activities, and youth programs. One of the best known of such centers is the Shiloh Baptist Church Family Life Center in Washington, D.C. Many black churches have also adopted aggressive programs to combat drugs and violence in their communities. The Church Takes A Corner (CTAC) Campaign is an example of one innovative approach by black churches. CTAC is a consortium of black churches in Wilmington, Delaware that mobilizes residents to eliminate open air drug markets by "occupying" various drug-trafficking corners in their community.

Black churches have historically assisted orphans and homeless children. Most of the early black orphanages were founded by black religious institutions. Recently, the disproportionate number of African American children in foster care has alarmed many ministers. The adoption of two adolescent black males in 1980 by a black Catholic priest, Father George Clement, of Holy Angels Church in Chicago, dramatized the plight of black children in foster care. Father Clement subsequently founded the One Church, One Child program to encourage each black church to make a commitment to adopt at least one foster child. Numerous coalitions of churches throughout the nation have adopted the One Church, One Child program. Furthermore, many black Catholic congregations across the nation have also implemented a broad range of programs to support black youth and their families.

Because of the persistent difficulty in attracting and retaining men, many black churches have adopted aggressive efforts to reach adolescent males.   The United Methodist Church in Chicago has established Big Brother/Male Mentors programs to provide positive male role models, especially for young men growing up in female-headed families.   Others, such as Union Temple Baptist Church in Washington, D.C., Trinity United Church of Christ in Chicago, and Bethel A.M.E. in Baltimore have a broad array of activities to appeal to young black males, including rites of passage programs to prepare them for the transition to manhood and responsible fatherhood.  Many Pentecostal and Christian charismatic churches also have innovative programs for increasing the involvement of young black males in productive pursuits.  While such programs are specifically targeted to unchurched young men, black churches also have many other programs that are targeted to young females.

The declining availability of affordable housing in the black community has also stimulated black churches to build housing for low-income families and senior citizens.  Examples of such churches include: Allen Temple Baptist Church in Oakland, California; Wheat Street Baptist Church in Atlanta, Georgia; Church of the Good Shepherd Congregational and Antioch Missionary Baptist Church, both in Chicago; United House of Prayer for All People in Washington, D.C.; and Bridge Street A.M.E. Church in Brooklyn, New York.

To revitalize entire neighborhoods, many black churches, such as First A.M.E. Church in Los Angeles, California, and Hartford Memorial Baptist Church in Detroit, Michigan, have formed community development corporations to stimulate the growth of black businesses and to increase the stock of affordable housing.  Zion Investment Corporation, a development arm of Zion Baptist Church in Philadelphia, has built a shopping center and created small businesses in such areas as construction, real estate, and wiring.   In addition, Zion's 32-year old Opportunities Industrialization Center (OIC), founded by its pastor, Reverend Leon Sullivan, is a nationally acclaimed employment program that has trained over 750,000 low-income residents for a wide variety of jobs (Sullivan 1969; Freedman 1993; Taylor 1994).

Similarly, in Washington, D.C., the United House of Prayer for All People has constructed McCullough Plaza--a huge development complex of housing, shopping facilities, and small businesses (Alexander 1987).   In

Miami, the St. John Community Development Corporation, established by St. John Baptist Church, is revitalizing that city's Overtown section--a low-income community that had been devastated by periodic waves of rioting during the 1980s. Finally, Allen A.M E. Church in Jamaica, New York, has established a housing corporation, a 300-unit senior citizens complex, a 480-pupil elementary school, a health-service facility, and a home-care agency for the elderly and handicapped. Lastly, BUILD, a coalition of churches in Baltimore from various denominations, have instituted a Nehemiah Project and other creative initiatives to revitalize inner-city communities (Woodson 1987; Reed 1994; Gite 1994).

To insure more effective use of the mammoth resources of the Black Church, the Congress of National Black Churches (CNBC) was formed as a coalition of eight major historically black denominations: African Methodist Episcopal; African Methodist Episcopal Zion; Christian Methodist Episcopal; Church of God in Christ; National Baptist Convention of America, Inc.; National Baptist Convention, USA, Inc; National Missionary Baptist Convention of America; and the Progressive National Baptist Convention, Inc. These denominations represent 65,000 churches and a membership of over 19 million persons. CNBC was founded in 1978 under the direction of Bishop John Hurst Adams and has its headquarters in Washington, D.C. Over the past two decades, CNBC has instituted innovative programs in such areas as church leadership development, child development programs (Project Spirit), community and economic development, crime and drug abuse prevention, and the strengthening of African American families.

# Chapter 9

# Summary and Implications

In this work, we have focused on factors in the wider society, the black community, black families, and among black individuals that enhance the social and economic functioning and resilience of African American families. In order to properly understand the functioning of African American families, we used a holistic or solutions perspective. This interdisciplinary framework highlighted historical research that focused on the outstanding legacy of achievements of blacks from dynasties in early Africa to current periods in America.

The new urban history revealed that blacks--both as slaves and freemen--were not passive objects of oppression but played major roles in their quest for freedom and equality. Historical research also revealed that although qualitative differences exist between the present and the past, many commonalities persist: (a) the higher levels of female-headed families and out-of-wedlock births among blacks than whites can be traced to the nineteenth century and are not unique to recent decades; and (b) "underclass" segments (such as alley families, slum dwellers, etc.) of the black community have a long history and are not peculiar to contemporary inner-city areas.

Moreover, according to recent anthropological and ethnographic research, many of the resiliency-producing values and successful coping strategies of contemporary black families are cultural strengths that are derived from their African legacy. In fact, cross-cultural studies of contemporary black families have found such patterns as extended families, informal adoption, high status of women, spirituality, and flexible family roles to be major contributors to the stabilization and upward mobility of African and Caribbean families.

Our holistic perspective also identified factors at the societal and community levels that undermined the stability of black families since the 1970s. Some of the key social forces that contributed to black family dysfunction include: institutional racism and sexism, shifts from high-paying manufacturing jobs to low-wage service economy, back-to-back recessions, increasing unemployment and poverty, the exporting of jobs from inner-cities and the importing of drugs and weapons, the soaring AIDS epidemic, the disparate arrests and incarceration of black men and women, decline in the availability of employment for males, and increases in out-of-wedlock births.

A major objective of this work was to identify protective factors at the individual, family, and community level that mediated or counteracted the negative effects of social forces and policies on African American families. We focused on the following five resiliency factors: achievement orientation, work orientation, flexible family roles, kinship bonds, and religious orientation.

Our review of studies revealed that a strong academic orientation has facilitated upward mobility for thousands of low-income blacks. Academic resiliency was enhanced by such factors as: high parental aspirations, high youth aspirations, high self-esteem, biculturalism, strong racial identity, balance between internal and external loci of control, and the role of black colleges. Despite increasing unemployment and work discouragement, many studies have found that most blacks continue to manifest a strong work orientation. Researchers have found that black youth have a strong work ethic and are more willing than white youth to accept low wages. Most importantly, most black adults prefer work over welfare.

The flexibility of family roles as a major protective factor was also examined. Such flexibility was manifested in: egalitarian family roles; the resilience of single-parent families; the rearing of boys by single mothers; the rearing of children by single fathers; and the resilience of black adolescents to substance abuse. Many studies of black families consistently reveal the continuing importance of kinship bonds against tremendous odds. Extended families--related and nonrelated--provide various kinds of support to black families: services to unwed teen mothers; day-care services to working parents; informal foster care and adoption; formal foster care and adoption; reduction of child abuse; and mutual social and economic assistance.

Many studies revealed that a strong religious orientation and spirituality are major contributors to enhancing the resilience of African American individuals and families. Youth with strong religious commitments are more likely to achieve upward mobility and engage in positive social behavior than youth with weak religious commitment. Black churches--in both urban and rural areas--continue to perform important social welfare and economic functions for disdadvantaged children, adults, and families. They are increasingly providing a wide range of support activities: tutoring, mentoring, soup kitchens, thrift shops, homeless shelters, parenting classes for single parents, AIDS and drug prevention, crime watch, construction of low-income housing, and establishing small businesses, etc.

## IMPLICATIONS

We will now discuss implications of these findings for public policies in the wider society and self-help initiatives in the African American community. In order to strengthen the functioning of black families throughout the 21st century and beyond, innovative public policies are needed in the broader society that complement and reinforce self-help efforts in the black community. First, we will briefly describe strategies required by institutions external to the black community and then conclude with an overview of self-help initiatives required in the black community.

## PUBLIC POLICIES

### Guiding Principles

To be effective, any public policies designed to enhance the functioning of African American families must incorporate three guiding principles: opposition to racism, family impact analyses, and appropriate targeting to groups and areas based on social and economic need. We will now briefly discuss each of these important principles.

### Opposition to Racism

Unfortunately, despite assertions about the declining significance of race, racism continues to be a major force impeding the progress and mobility of people and families of color. Racism by individuals is still pervasive in our society, but structural discrimination by American institutions appears to be more widespread and invidious. A recent example of institutional racism was passage of a cocaine disparity act by Congress in 1995, which will result in the incarceration of more blacks than whites. Offenders who possess crack cocaine (who are mostly black) will receive more severe sentences than offenders who possess the same or larger amounts of powder cocaine (who are mostly white), despite the equally harmful effects of both types of cocaine.

Civil rights organizations must make greater use of existing legal remedies to counteract structural discrimination and other forms of institutional racism. The basic precedent has been the *Griggs v. Duke Power Company* decree (1971), in which the U.S. Supreme Court declared the company's employment tests unconstitutional and discriminatory because of their "disparate adverse impact" on hiring minority workers, even though such consequences were unintentional. The U.S. Congress overwhelmingly inserted the "effects" standard in its renewal of the Voting Rights Act of 1982 to ensure that consequences, not intent, would be the overriding criterion for determining the constitutionality of specific electoral processes. In short, successful court challenges can be mounted against institutionally discriminatory policies that disproportionately impact individuals and families of color, even if those effects were not originally intended.

### Family Impact Analyses

A major impediment to strengthening families is the fact that most public policies are targeted to individuals and not families. Policies that are focused on families are often not effective because they are fragmented and have rules and regulations that are inconsistent with other policies. What is vitally needed are comprehensive and coordinated policies that provide important assistance and support to individuals within a family context.

Interestingly, the government mandates that studies be conducted of the impact of public policies on the environment, especially on natural resources and endangered animals, but no similar impact analyses are required for people or families. We think there is a need for systematic analyses of the potential and actual impact of social policies on families from various ethnic and class backgrounds. Policies that are shown to have disparate adverse effects on minority families, for example, should be changed to eliminate any negative consequences. Government impact analyses on families should incorporate the criteria recommended by the Family Impact Seminar, a national policy center, to assess the intended and unintended effects of public policies on families.

### Effective Targeting

Record-level budget deficits, trade deficits, and periodic recessions suggest an austere economic climate in the 21st century that will require policies that are cost effective and more effectively targeted to the racially and economically disadvantaged individuals and families. Communities with the highest levels of social and economic problems are disproportionately concentrated among racial and ethnic minorities who live in low-income urban and rural communities. Such communities should be targeted for a comprehensive array of programs and services. Empowerment Zones and Enterprise Communities, which were established in 1995, are the kind of targeted policies that are needed to concentrate public and private resources for economic development in disadvantaged cities and rural areas (Hill 1992; Thomas and Ritzdorf 1997).

## Stimulating Economic Growth

Many analysts contend that an expanding economy contributes significantly to economic progress among black families and that economic growth helps to reduce racial inequality. Consequently, the black community must insist that government policies to reduce inflation no longer rely on inducing recessions, which ultimately raise unemployment levels. Moreover, since small businesses generate the largest numbers of new jobs in the American economy, additional government resources and set asides should be targeted to increase the number and effectiveness of small minority businesses in low-income communities (Wilson 1996).

## Full Employment

This nation must rededicate itself to the goals of the Employment Act of 1946 and the Humphrey-Hawkins Act of 1978 to provide everyone willing and able to work with jobs at livable wages. Current tax credits that subsidize the exporting of American jobs abroad should be reversed to provide greater incentives for creating decent jobs at home. Livable wages will not be achieved until the federal minimum is made commensurate with the cost of living. Legislation passed by Congress in July 1996, which raised the minimum wage from $4.25 to $4.75 an hour in 1996 and to $5.15 an hour in 1997, is an important step toward that goal.

## Expanding Subsidized Jobs

Contrary to conventional wisdom, analyses of the public service programs, especially those under the Comprehensive Employment and Training Act (CETA) created by the Nixon Administration in the early 1970s, reveal that they were effective in facilitating the transition of low-income and minority workers to higher-paying, unsubsidized jobs in the private sector (Hill 1981).  Consequently, additional funding should be provided for subsidized public service jobs and subsidized on-the-job training in the private sector that is targeted to unemployed workers in low-income families.  More effective marketing of the Targeted Jobs Tax Credits (TJTC) to firms, combined with changes to reduce their stigma among participants, would markedly increase the number of disadvantaged youth and welfare recipients hired at subsidized wages through TJTC.

### Expanding Child Care

A major barrier to labor force participation by many single parents, especially blacks, is the lack of affordable child care.  Unfortunately, the Dependent Care Tax Credit (DCTC) is not used by most working poor parents because their incomes are too low to incur tax liabilities.  The amount of the DCTC should be increased and made refundable, similar to the Earned Income Tax Credit (EITC), to insure that working poor families receive tax rebates for child care, even when they do not have to pay taxes. However, in order to confront this issue on a more comprehensive basis, this nation must give serious consideration to implementing a children's allowance, similar to those in many European countries, so that thousands of families with young children may be lifted out of poverty.

### Reforming AFDC

President Clinton's signing of the Personal Responsibility and Work Opportunity Reconciliation Act of 1996 on 22, August 1996 terminated a sixty-year commitment by the federal government to play a major role in providing cash and in-kind assistance to poor and needy individuals and families.  This welfare reform (or "repeal") ended the open-ended entitlements for poor families with dependent children and devolved primary responsibility for welfare to states through two block grants.  One block grant, Block Grants to States for Temporary Assistance for Needy Families (TANF), is designed to help welfare recipients leave the rolls within specified time limits: two years to obtain jobs, and a maximum of five years to receive welfare benefits.  Although the second block grant is designed to provide subsidized child care for welfare recipients who are able to obtain jobs, many observers predict that the funds are inadequate for the large number of recipients who will need child care assistance.

Unfortunately, there are a number of major weaknesses in the 1996 Act: (1) It has fixed amounts that will not be responsive to economic downturns and periodic recessions; (2) It has inadequate resources for providing extended training and education to enhance the capabilities of "long-term" recipients with few marketable skills; (3) It will place most recipients into short-term, low-wage jobs with no health benefits; (4) It has inadequate funds to provide subsidized child care for the large numbers of recipients who are expected to find jobs; (5) It relies on churches and other nonprofit institutions to provide increased assistance to the poor with limited government resources; and (6) It is likely to increase the number of persons who are homeless, poor, and in foster care.

Unless radical changes are made, this act is not likely to increase the self-sufficiency of most welfare recipients, nor will it lift most of them out of poverty. To achieve genuine welfare reform, state governments and welfare recipients must agree to fulfill mutual obligations. Since most low-paying jobs that welfare recipients would obtain do not provide health benefits, medical assistance, and, especially, subsidized child care would be needed for a reasonable transitional period while they are employed. Additionally, policies that help welfare recipients increase their education and work skills have a greater chance of enhancing their long-term economic independence. A progressive model for welfare reform was implemented by the Department of Social Services in Anne Arundel County, Maryland prior to passage of the 1996 legislation.

## Enhancing Child Support

The 1996 Welfare Act also includes provisions for increased enforcement of child-support collection by improving procedures for paternity establishment, for locating absent parents, and for withholding wages and tax refunds. Nevertheless, many inequities continue to exist in current child-support policies, such as inadequate levels of child support awards ordered by courts, sharp disparities between the amount of child support ordered and the ability to pay, harsher punishment for low-income than middle-income noncustodial fathers, and little recognition of noncustodial fathers who provide regular in-kind support. Policies are needed that encourage, and not discourage, responsible noncustodial parents to make regular child support payments, provide social and emotional support, and to have regular child visitations. More government resources should be provided to encourage low-income and jobless noncustodial fathers to participate in GED classes and obtain job training to enhance their employability.

## Enhancing Foster Care and Adoption

Interestingly, during the welfare reform debate, several congressmen suggested that the children of welfare recipients (who are removed from the rolls for not finding jobs) be placed in orphanages. This is one of the few times that discussions of welfare reform refer to the foster-care system. Yet, it is curious why these same legislators do not propose placing the half-million children currently in foster care into orphanages if they are such desirable settings. Obviously, the prohibitive costs of such placement is why most of the children continue to remain in families. However, genuine reform of the foster-care system is urgently needed.

A major advance was made in 1980 with passage of the Adoption Assistance and Child Welfare Act (PL 96-272). For the first time, this legislation linked foster-care services with child welfare, set a timetable for periodic review of children in foster care, and assigned high priority to family preservation services to reduce unnecessary placement of children in foster care. Unfortunately, because this act did not receive sufficient funding, it was never implemented as originally designed. The soaring number of children in foster care, many of them from alcohol-addicted, drug-addicted, and AIDS-infected parents make reform of the foster-care system an urgent necessity. Although a provision in the 1996 Welfare Reform Act encourages interracial adoptions while deemphasizing same-race placements, it will primarily affect the adoption of healthy black infants who are the easiest to adopt. The older, hard-to-adopt children will continue to wait for long periods of time.

We urge the following strategies for enhancing culturally sensitive foster care and adoption placements:

(a) Restore funds to the 1980 Act to permit adequate implementation across the nation;

(b) Place a major priority on family-preservation services, since they have demonstrated their effectiveness in reducing unnecessary placements;

(c) Mandate traditional adoption agencies to establish goals and timetables for hiring more minority workers and insuring that all of their workers receive regular cultural sensitivity training;

(d) Establish "kinship care" as a unique resource for placement with adequate funding to kin caregivers;

(e)   provide more resources to permit low-income foster parents to become adoptive parents; and

(f)   support the establishment and licensing of community- based agencies operated by racial and ethnic groups that have demonstrated their effectiveness in finding permanent homes for children of color.

We strongly support policies that place priority on same-race, same-culture adoption placements and oppose policies (such as the 1994 Multiethnic Placement Act and the 1996 Welfare Reform Act) that deemphasize such placements. We also urge that serious consideration be given to policies implemented by several states, such as Michigan, that provide higher financial incentives to agencies that place foster children in adoptive or permanent homes within relatively short time periods than to agencies that permit children to languish for long time spans.

## Enhancing Education

The quality of education for children of color in public schools must be enhanced markedly. The school restructuring movement toward site-based management that is culturally sensitive should be encouraged. We strongly recommend that more school systems try to achieve the characteristics of "effective schools" identified by noted educational administrator, the late Ronald Edmonds, to strengthen inner-city schools: clear and focused missions, instructional leadership, high expectations of success for all students, safe and orderly environment, regular monitoring of student progress, many learning opportunities, and strong home-school relations that encourage active parent involvement. We also believe that serious efforts should be made to provide more private school options for low-income parents.

A disturbing trend has been recent declines in college enrollment of black students--both male and female. These declines suggest that the growth of the black middle class may slow considerably during the coming decades because access to a college education has been the primary vehicle for blacks to achieve class mobility and improved occupational opportunities. A major contributor to such decline has been the sharp reduction in scholarships and other financial assistance to low-income students who want to go to college. Since increasing numbers of black students and their families are forced to rely on loans, they often complete their college education with extensive debts that are equivalent to mortgages on homes. Obviously, many low-income youth decide not to attend college in order to avoid being saddled with such financial burdens. Clearly, there is a vital need to increase funding for Pell Grants and other scholarships for low-income students.

Furthermore, additional funds should be targeted to strengthen historically black colleges, since they continue to produce disproportionate numbers of black college graduates. Although students at black colleges comprise less than 20 percent of all blacks who attend college, they produce the majority of blacks who complete college. Moreover, while enrollment in many predominantly white institutions is decreasing, enrollment in many predominantly black institutions continues to rise. Many of the students who choose to attend predominantly black colleges have SAT scores that would easily qualify them to attend predominantly white colleges. Thus, historically black colleges continue to be a lifeline for thousands of low-income youth who would never go to college, as well as for middle-income youth who want a quality education and a supportive, predominantly black, college environment.

## Enhancing Health

The proliferation of drug abuse and HIV/AIDS will continue to be major health concerns for inner cities in the 21st century. More government resources must be allocated for substance abuse and AIDS prevention and treatment programs. Lack of quality health care is a key contributor to persistent high rates of poverty, welfare, dependency, and infant mortality among blacks. The lack of health benefits in low-wage jobs has acutely affected the black working poor. There is a vital need for comprehensive national health insurance (including portable coverage from job to job) that is targeted to the welfare poor, working poor, and working near-poor. Aggressive action is also needed to reduce the high rates of adolescent pregnancy, infant mortality, poor prenatal care, low birth-weight babies, AIDS-infected parents and infants, and drug-addicted parents and infants in the black community. Additional government funds are urgently needed to provide adequate treatment and support services to drug-addicted and HIV/AIDS-infected individuals and families. Furthermore, more resources should also be provided to assist the thousands of children who are left behind as a result of the death of their parents to drugs and AIDS.

## Enhancing Youth Development

A broad range of initiatives at the national and community levels are needed to enhance the development of African American and youth (Mincy 1994; Taylor 1995). Yet, national youth-oriented policies must shift from viewing minority youth as "problems" to recognizing them as "resources" for making productive contributions to society. Major areas of priority for empowering youth should include educational development, work and career preparation, personal development, and family bonding. In order to increase the effectiveness of their services, national youth-serving groups (such as the Boys Scouts, Girls Scouts, YMCAs, YWCAs, Boys and Girls Clubs, NAACP, National Urban League, etc.) must coordinate their activities with one another. Additional resources should be provided to strengthen community-based groups that serve minority youth. However, as Courtland Lee (1994) and Morris Jeff (1994) observe, successful programs for African American youth must be sensitive to their cultural traditions and promote positive racial identity. Clearly, more Afrocentric program models, including rites of passage programs, are needed to empower African American youth and their parents. Culturally sensitive programs are also needed to enhance the development of high-risk youth who have come into contact with the criminal justice and foster-care systems. Serious consideration should be given to passage of Youth Development Block Grants to strengthen the activities of youth-servicing organizations at national and community levels.

## Reducing Crime and Violence

Crime and violence continue to be serious problems for all communities in America--urban and rural, inner cities and suburbs, and in large and small cities. The exporting of jobs and the importing of drugs and weapons are major factors in destabilizing many black families. Many inner-city communities are in a state of siege: innocent children and adults are wounded or killed as a result of drive-by shootings, and many persons, especially seniors, are "prisoners" in their homes. Aggressive responses are needed by federal, state, and local law enforcement agencies as well as courts. We also call for an end to the differential sentencing of crack and powder cocaine offenders, and urge that offenders should receive equal sentences for possessing similar amounts of drugs. Moreover, the charge based on the carefully-researched "Dark Alliance" series by Gary Webb

(1996) that the Central Intelligence Agency (CIA) aided and abetted the importing of drugs and weapons into South Central Los Angeles should not be casually dismissed as has been done by the mainstream media. We urge the appointment of a special prosecutor or a presidential commission of citizens to investigate allegations that the CIA, the Drug Enforcement Agency (DEA), and other law enforcement agencies might be directly or indirectly responsible for thousands of deaths in inner cities as a result of drug-related violence since the mid-1980s.    More community policing approaches are needed in which local police work closely with citizens to combat crime and violence in their areas.    More resources should be directed to expand effective anti-violence initiatives, such as the Minority-Male Consortium comprising nineteen historically black colleges and universities (HBCUs). Additional recreational facilities should be established in many inner-city communities to provide wholesome activities for low-income children and youth.

**Enhancing Public Housing**

Pubic housing residents in many cities across the nation have demonstrated that they can manage and rehabilitate their developments more cost effectively than local authorities and reduce welfare dependency and crime in the process (Woodson, 1987; Williams and Kornblum, 1994). The  Kenilworth-Parkside's  Resident  Management  Corporation  in Washington, D.C., has restored community pride by creating over a dozen small businesses and sending over six hundred children to college.  More resources should be targeted to: (a) training resident councils in housing management; (b) helping public housing residents to form community development corporations to renovate their facilities; and (c) assisting public housing residents who wish to become homeowners.

**Expanding Low-Income Housing**

The critical shortage of affordable housing for low-income families has led to an alarming surge in overcrowding, homelessness, foster- care placement, child neglect, family violence, and physical and mental illness. The government must renew its commitment to provide quality and affordable housing to all individuals and families in need.  There is an urgent need to expand the availability of subsidized rental units, renovate thousands of abandoned and boarded-up homes, and expand home-ownership options for low-income families through urban homesteading, sweat equity, and other forms of self-help.  There is also a need for more effective enforcement of the 1977 Community Reinvestment Act (CRA) in inner cities and the expansion of lending for community development.

## SELF-HELP INITIATIVES

Public and private sectors policy strategies to enhance the functioning of African American families should complement, not undermine, self-help efforts of the black community.  In order to have strong families, we must have strong communities.  Thus, the overriding goal of black self-help efforts should be the strengthening and building of strong social and economic institutions in the African American community.  To achieve that goal, black individuals, families and organizations must empower themselves socially, economically and politically.  The total African American community must rededicate itself in the spirit of the historic "day of atonement" on 16 October 1995 in Washington, D.C. and make a deeper commitment to implement the seven principles of the Nguzo Saba on a daily basis.  The strategies required to achieve these objectives include conducting capacity surveys and tapping the resources of black churches, black colleges, national black organizations, community-based organizations and individuals.

### Capacity Surveys

In many inner cites, needs assessment surveys are usually conducted to identify deficiencies, since it is popularly assumed that people who reside in low-income black communities or neighborhoods have no assets, capacities, or talents.  Thus, many residents of disadvantaged communities are labeled as "welfare recipients," "teen mothers," "drug addicts," "delinquents," "criminals," or "deadbeat dads," etc.  Capacity surveys of low-income communities, however, have revealed that all residents have some talents, assets, and strengths.  The unsung talents of these mislabeled people serve as important protective mechanisms for enhancing the resilience of many low-income children and families.  Robert Woodson refers to such inner-city individuals and groups as "community healers" and "antibodies. . . .because they work in communities in just the way antibodies work in the human organism.  What we need to do is to find ways to strengthen these little cells of health and organize them into an immune system" (Raspberry, 1996).

Capacity surveys conducted by the Northwestern University Center for Urban Affairs and Policy Research have found a wide range of capabilities among low-income residents. These talents include: cooking, sewing, child care, cosmetology, barbering, music, carpentry, electrician, repairman, sports, health care, tutoring, mentoring, surrogate parenting, etc. Each day, such talents are used to help thousands of inner-city children, youth, adults, and families to achieve against the odds (Kretzmann and McKnight 1993).

**Black Churches**

In the 21st century, the Black Church will have to reaffirm its historic role as the preeminent black institution for strengthening the social and economic functioning of African American children, youth, and families (Freedman 1993; Gite 1994). Deep budget cuts and the transformation of federal funds to state block grants for social welfare services will enhance the role of private organizations, especially churches, in providing a broad range of human services to needy individuals and families. The decentralization of government functions will increase the need for greater involvement of religious institutions in strengthening families, developing housing, creating small businesses, and other community enhancement and economic development activities.

**Black Colleges**

Historically black colleges and universities should be used increasingly as important resources for strengthening families and revitalizing African American communities. HBCUs should be strengthened to perform their historic role of providing access to quality higher education for thousands of low-income and middle-income black students. In addition, innovative HUD community and economic development programs for HBCUs should be expanded and supported by other public and private agencies to encourage HBCUs to: (a) form and/or assist community development corporations (CDCs); (b) develop low-income housing; (d) assist in forming black businesses; (e) provide vital services to low-income children and families; and (f) provide vocational and technical training to enhance job opportunities of inner-city residents. Such colleges should also play major roles in model program demonstrations and in conducting research and evaluation studies on many key issues. The HHS-funded consortium of HBCUs to combat violence and drug abuse on-campus and off-campus should be continued and replicated as a model of partnership between government agencies and black colleges. Additional resources are needed to strengthen effective violence-prevention programs, such as the Morgan State University Family Life Center's Alternative to Violence Program (AVP), and the Coppin State College Project BRAVE, both of which enhance the conflict resolution and peer resistance skills of inner-city youth.

## National Black Organizations

National black groups, such as the NAACP, National Urban League, National Council of Negro Women, National African American Leadership Summit, Nation of Islam, Southern Christian Leadership Conference, Congress of National Black Churches, National Black Child Development Institute, fraternal groups, professional associations and caucuses, etc., need to coordinate their various activities to provide more effective strategies for improving the African American community. The Black Congressional Caucus needs to aggressively implement Ossie Davis's plea at its inaugural dinner, "It's the plan, not the man." The Black Caucus should expand its "Brain Trust" concept by sponsoring or stimulating research and evaluation studies on major policy issues by black scholars from a broad range of disciplines. Moreover, black national organizations need to communicate more frequently with community-based black groups, perhaps through Internet home pages, to mobilize nationwide to support or oppose various public or private actions.

## Community-Based Organizations

The role of community-based organizations (CBOs) has increased in importance in African American communities throughout the nation. Resident management corporations, for example, demonstrate that public housing residents can maintain safe, pleasant, and comfortable living environments more efficiently and cost effectively than local public housing authorities (Williams 1987). Many neighborhood groups are implementing innovative tutoring, mentoring, rites of passage, and entrepreneurship programs for inner-city youth and providing vital social and economic support for adult and teen single-parents and couples (Gilbert and Tyehimba-Taylor 1993; Mincy 1994). Numerous Local Organizing Committees (LOCs) are implementing the goals of the Million Man March by instituting a wide range of community and economic development activities that are designed to strengthen black adult males and females, children, and families.

Neighborhood groups have also shown their effectiveness in enhancing the quality of life of their residents. Community crime watches and other safety patrols have aided community policing efforts by reducing crime and drug trafficking in their areas. Nation of Islam security patrols have dramatically reduced crime and drug trafficking in inner cities across the nation. Numerous faith-based community groups are demonstrating each day that they are vital "antibodies" in providing services to combat many so-called intractable problems, such as alcoholism, drug addiction, teen pregnancies, inadequate work skills, welfare dependency, etc. But these neighborhood groups need more resources from the public and private sectors to more effectively reach the thousands of low-income children, adults and families who vitally need their services.

### Caring Individuals

Yet, the most frequent self-help providers are individuals, not community groups or national organizations. There are thousands of "unsung heroes" throughout this nation who provide vital support and encouragement to children, youth, elderly, and families. Such individuals are parents, grandparents, aunts, uncles, brothers, sisters, nieces, nephews, grandchildren, other relatives, friends, and neighbors. About ten years ago, JET magazine conducted a poll to identify individuals who help other people without using government funds (Booker 1986). The poll identified couples who cared for 350 foster children over twenty-two years; individuals who provided programs for senior citizens in their homes; a social worker who has helped more then twenty young people to attend college; couples who have tutored more than sixty children in their homes; and other individuals who provide assistance to children, youth, unwed teenagers, single parents, and the homeless. Other examples are Bea Gaddy in Baltimore and Deloris Sims in Chicago who feed hundreds of needy families and homeless individuals each year; Reverend Imagene Stewart who founded the House of Imagene in Washington, D.C. over twenty years ago as one of the first shelters for battered black women in this nation; and Mr. and Mrs. Kent Amos in Washington, D.C. who have reared over fifty children in their home without any government funds. These individuals demonstrate the strengths of black families in their daily lives and should be emulated by many others in the African American village.

## Future Research

Although we have made many recommendations for future research throughout this work, we would like to conclude by highlighting some suggestions for studies on black families. Many of the findings discussed in this work are based on studies by white and black social scientists from a broad array of disciplines--historians, sociologists, anthropologists, ethnographers, social workers, psychologists, psychiatrists, philosophers, economists, etc. Although many of these studies are not often cited in public discussions of blacks because their findings do not support popular stereotypes, they have contributed important new insights into the structure and functioning of families of color. We strongly urge similar studies of the strengths and resilience of families of color by scholars from various ethnic and racial groups. In short, greater priority should be given to understanding why so many low-income people of color are able to become successful in spite of racial and class barriers. Why do black youth, for example, more often have lower rates of substance abuse than white youth? Why are black youth from female-headed families more likely to engage in pro-social behavior than white youth from female-headed families?

There is a need for studies of black families that simultaneously examine the effects on family functioning of factors at the societal, community, family, and individual levels. Such studies would also require research that cuts across disciplines and fields. Furthermore, there should be more ethnographic studies of families of color. Many important black family processes and dynamics can be investigated more effectively through qualitative rather than quantitative studies.

Finally, there needs to be less emphasis on blacks as passive victims of external forces and more assessments of people of color as major change agents in enhancing their well-being.

# BIBLIOGRAPHY

Alexander, Bill. 1987. "The Black Church and Community Empowerment."
Pp. 45-69 in *On the Road to Economic Freedom*, ed. Robert L. Woodson.
Washington, DC: Regnery Gateway.

Allen, Walter R. 1976. "The Family Antecedents of Adolescent Mobility
Aspirations." *Journal of Afro-American Issues* 4 (3-4): 295-314.

_____. 1978. "The Search for Applicable Theories of Black Family Life." *Journal of
Marriage and the Family* 40 (1): 117-29.

Anderson, Claud. 1994. *Black Labor, White Wealth.* Edgewood, MD: Duncan and
Duncan.

Angell, Robert C. 1936. *The Family Encounters the Depression.* New York: Charles
Scribner & Sons.

Aschenbrenner, Joyce. 1975. *Lifelines: Black Families in Chicago.* New York: Holt,
Reinhart and Winston.

Auletta, Ken. 1982. *The Underclass.* New York: Random House.

Bachman, Jerold G. 1970. *Youth in Transition: Volume II. The Impact of Family
Background and Intelligence on Tenth Grade Boys.* Ann Arbor, MI: University
of Michigan. Institute for Social Research.

Bachrach, Christine. 1983. "Adoption as a Means of Family Formation: Data from
the National Survey of Family Growth." *Journal of Marriage and the Family*
45 (4): 859-65.

Baratz, Steven S. and Joan Baratz. 1970. "Early Childhood Intervention: The Social
Science Base of Institutional Racism." *Harvard Educational Review* 40 (1): 29-50.

Barnard, Henry. 1871. (1969 Reprint). *History of Schools for the Colored Population.*
New York: Arno Press.

Benson, Peter L. and Michael J. Donahue. 1989. "Ten-Year Trends in At-Risk
Behaviors." *Journal of Adolescent Research* 4 (2): 125-39.

Benson, Peter and Eugene C. Roehlkepartain. 1993."Youth in Single-Parent
Families: Risk and Resiliency." Search Institute Background Paper.

Bergdorf, K. 1981. "Recognition and Reporting of Child Maltreatment: Findings
from the National Study of the Incidence and Severity of Child Abuse and
Neglect." Washington, DC: National Center on Child Abuse and Neglect.

Berrick, Jill and Richard P. Barth, eds. 1994. "Kinship Foster Care." *Children and
Youth Service Review* 16 (2) (Special Double Issue)

Berry, Gordon and Claudia Mitchell-Kernan, eds. 1982. *Television and the
Socialization of the Minority Child.* New York: Academic Press.

Berry, Mary F. and John W. Blassingame. 1982. *Long Memory: The Black
Experience in America.* New York: Oxford University Press.

Billingsley, Andrew. 1968. *Black Families in White America.* Englewood Cliffs, NJ:
Prentice-Hall.

_____. 1973. "Black Family Structure: Myths and Realities." In *Studies in Public Welfare, Part II.* Washington, DC: U.S. Congress Joint Economic Committee, 306-19.

_____. 1992. *Climbing Jacob's Ladder.* New York: Simon & Schuster.

_____. ed. 1994. "The Black Church." *National Journal of Sociology* 8 (1-2). (Double edition)

Blascovich, J. and J. Tomaka. 1991. "Measures of Self-Esteem." Pp. 115-60 in *Measures of Personalty and Psychosocial Attitudes,* ed. J. P. Robinson, P. R. Shaver, and L. S. Wrightsman. New York: Academic Press.

Blassingame, John W. 1973. *Black New Orleans, 1860-1880.* Chicago, IL: University of Chicago Press.

Bluestone, Barry and Bernard Harrison. 1982. *The Deindustrialization of America.* New York: Basic Books.

Booker, Simeon. 1986. "Poll Reveals Blacks Who Aid Blacks and Don't Ask U.S. Help." *Jet* (18 August), 10-12.

Borchert, James. 1980. *Alley Life in Washington.* Chicago, IL: University of Illinois Press.

Borus, Michael. 1980. "Willingness to Work." In *Pathways to the Future: A Longitudinal Study of Young Americans.* Columbus, OH: Ohio State University, Center for Human Resources Research.

Bowman, Phillip J. 1995. "Commentary on Darity and Myers, 'Family Structure and the Marginalization of Black Men: Policy Implications.'" Pp. 263-308 in *The Decline in Marriage Among African Americans.* New York: Russell Sage Foundation.

_____. 1993. "The Impact of Economic Marginality Among African-American Husbands and Fathers." Pp. 120-137 in *Family Ethnicity,* ed. Harriette P. McAdoo. Newbury Park, CA: Sage Publications.

_____. 1990. "Coping with Provider Role Strain: Cultural Resources Among Black Husband-Fathers." *Journal of Black Psychology* 16: 1-22.

_____. 1988. "Post-Industrial Displacment and Family Role Strain: Challenges to the Black Family." Pp. 75-97 in *Families and Economic Distress,* ed. P. Voydanof and L. C. Majka. Newbury Park, CA: Sage Publications.

Bowman, Phillip J. and Cleopatra S. Howard. 1985. "Race-Related Socialization, Motivation, and Academic Achievement: A Study of Black Youth in Three-Generation Families." *Journal of the American Academy of Child Psychiatry* 24 (2): 134-41.

Boyd-Franklin, Nancy. 1989. *Black Families in Therapy.* New York: Guilford Press.

Boykin, A. Wade and Forrest Toms. 1985. "Black Child Socialization." Pp. 35-51 in *Black Children,* ed. H. P. McAdoo and J. L. McAdoo. Beverly Hills, CA: Sage Publications.

Braithwaite, Ronald L. and Sandra E. Taylor, eds. 1992. *Health Issues and The Black Community.* San Francisco, CA: Josey-Bass Publishers.

Brashears, Freda and Margaret Roberts. 1996. "The Black Church as a Resource for Change." Pp. 181-192 in *The Black Family*, ed. Sadye Logan. Boulder, CO: Westview Press.

Brenner, M. Harvey. 1992. "Personal Stability and Economic Security." *Social Policy* 8 (1): 2-4.

Brim, Jr., Orville. 1957. "The Parent-Child Relation as a Social System: Parent and Child Roles." *Child Development* 28 (3), 345-46.

Bronfenbrenner, Urie. 1979. *The Ecology of Human Development*. Cambridge, MA: Harvard University Press.

Browder, Anthony T. 1989. *Nile Valley Contributions to Civilization. Vol. 1.* Washington, DC: The Institute of Karmic Guidance.

Brown, Sterling. 1937. "The Negro in Washington." Pp. 68-90 in *Washington: City and Capital*. Washington, DC: U.S. Government Printing Office.

Bryce-Laporte, Roy S. 1973. "Black Immigrants." Pp. 44-61 in *Through Different Eyes*, ed. Peter Rose et al. New York: Oxford University Press.

____. 1980. *Sourcebook on the New Immigration*. New Brunswick, NJ: Transaction Books.

Bryce-Laporte, Roy and Doris Mortimer, eds. 1973. *Caribbean Immigration in the United States*. Washington, DC: Smithsonian Institution.

Bullard, Robert D. 1990. *Dumping in Dixie*. Boulder, Co: Westview Press.

Bundles, A'Lelia P. 1991. *Madame C. J. Walker: Entrepreneur*. New York: Chelsea House Publishers.

Burgess, Ernest W. and Harvey J. Locke. 1945. *The Family: From Institution to Companionship*. New York: American Book Company.

Burton, Linda M. 1992. "Black Grandparents Rearing Children of Drug-Addicted Parents," *The Gerontologist* 32 (6): 744-51.

____. 1995. "Family Structure and Nonmarital Fertility: Perspectives for Ethnographic Research." Pp. 147-65 in *Report to Congress on Out-of-Wedlock Childbearing*. Washington, DC: National Center for Health Statistics.

Burton, Linda, Peggye Dilworth-Anderson, and Cynthia Merriwether-de Vries. 1995. "Context and Surrogate Parenting Among Contemporary Grandparents," *Marriage and Family Review* 20 (3-4): 349-66.

Carmichael, Stokely and Charles Hamilton. 1967. *Black Power*. New York: Vintage Books.

Carson, Ben. 1990. *Gifted Hands*. New York: Harper Paperbacks.

Carson, Emmett D. 1987. "Survey Dispels Myth That Blacks Receive, But Do Not Give to Charity." *Focus* 15 (March): 5.

Cauchon, Dennis. 1993. "Cocaine Sentencing Disparities Weighed." *USA Today* (10 November), 10-A.

Cavan, Ruth S. 1942. "Crises in Family Life." *The Family: Part 3*. New York: Thomas Y. Crowell Co.

Cazenave, Noel A. and Murray A. Straus. 1979. "Race, Class, Network Embeddedness and Family Violence: A Search for Potent Support Systems." *Journal of Comparative Family Studies* 10 (3): 281-300.

Cheatham, Harold E. and James B. Stewart, eds. 1990. *Black Families: Interdisciplinary Perspectives*. New Brunswick, NJ: Transaction Publishers.

Child Trends, Inc. 1989. *U.S. Children and Their Families: Current Conditions and Recent Trends, 1989*: A report prepared for the U.S. House of Representatives, Select Committee on Children, Youth and Families. 101st Cong., 1st Sess. (September) Washington, DC: Government Printing Office.

Clark, Reginald M. 1983. *Family Life and School Achievement: Why Poor Black Children Succeed and Fail*. Chicago: University of Chicago Press.

Clark, Kenneth B. and Mamie K. Clark. 1947. "Racial Identification and Preference in Children." Pp 169-87 in *Readings in Social Psychology*, ed. T. M. Newcomb and E. L. Hartley. New York: Holt, Rinehart, and Winston.

Clark-Lewis, Elizabeth. 1994. *Living In, Living Out, African American Domestics in Washington, D.C.: 1910-1940*. Washington, DC: Smithsonian Institution.

Cohen, D'Vera. 1994. "Blacks Bear Brunt of D.C.'s Pollution, Report Says."*Washington Post* (14 June), B-1, 3.

Coleman, James S. et al. 1966. *Equality of Educational Opportunity*. Washington, DC: U.S. Department of Health, Education and Welfare.

Commission on Racial Justice. 1987. *Toxic Wastes and Race*. New York: United Church of Christ.

Consortium for Research on Black Adolescence, ed. 1990. *Black Adolescence: Current Issues and Annotated Bibliography*. Boston, MA: G. K. Hall.

Coontz, Stephanie. 1992. *The Way We Never Were: American Families and the Nostalgia Trap*. New York: Basic Books.

Cox, Oliver C. 1976. *Race Relations*. Detroit, MI: Wayne University Press.

Cross, Jr., William E. 1983. "The Ecology of Human Development of Black and White Children:Implicationsfor Predicting Racial Preference Patterns." *Critical Perspectives of Third World America* 1 (1): 177-89.

_____. 1985. "Black Identity: Rediscovering the Distinction Between Personal Identity and Reference Group Orientation." Pp. 155-71 in *Beginnings: The Social and Affective Development of Black Children*, ed. M. B. Spencer, G. Kearse-Brookins, and W. R. Allen. Hillsdale, NJ: Lawrence Erlbaum.

_____. 1991. *Shades of Black: Diversity in African-American Identity*. Philadelphia, PA: Temple University Press.

Cummings, Scott. 1997. "Explaining Poor Academic Performance Among Black Children." *Educational Forum* 41 (3): 335-46.

Curry, Leonard P. 1981. *The Free Black in Urban America, 1800-1850*. Chicago, IL: University of Chicago Press.

Darity, Jr., William A. and Samuel L. Myers, Jr. 1995. "Family Structure and the Marginalization of Black Men."Pp. 309-21 in *The Decline in Marriage Among African Americans*, ed. M. Belinda Tucker and Claudia Mitchell-Kernan. New York: Russell Sage Foundation.

Della, Jr., M. Ray. 1973. "An Analysis of Baltimore's Population in the 1850's." *Maryland Historical Magazine* 68 (1): 20-35.

Delpit, Lisa. 1995. *Other People's Children: Cultural Conflict in the Classroom.* New York: The New Press.

Dembo, Richard. 1988. "Delinquency Among Black Male Youth." Pp. 129-65 in *Young, Black, and Male in America*, ed. Jewelle T. Gibbs. Dover, MA: Auburn House.

Denby, Ramona W. 1996. "Resiliency and the African American Family: A Model of Family Preservation." Pp. 144-163 in *The Black Family*, ed. Sadye L. Logan. Boulder, CO: Westview Press.

Dickerson, Bette J., ed. 1995. *African-American Single Mothers: Understanding Their Lives and Families.* Thousand Oaks, CA: Sage Publications.

Dill, Bonnie T. 1980. "The Means to Put My Children Through: Child-Rearing Goals and Strategies Among Black Female Domestic Servants." Pp. 107-23 in *The Black Woman*, ed. La Frances Rodgers-Rose. Beverly Hills, CA: Sage Publications.

____. 1994. *Beyond the Boundaries of Race and Class: An Exploration of Work and Family Among Black Female Domestic Servants.* New York: Garland Publishers.

Diop, Cheikh Anta. 1991. *Civilization or Barbarism.* Brooklyn, New York: Lawrence Hill Books.

Dixon, Vernon J. and Badi Foster, eds. 1971. *Beyond Black and White.* Boston, MA: Little, Brown & Co.

Downs, Anthony. 1970. "Racism in America and How to Combat It." Pp. 5-114 in *Urban Problems and Prospects*, ed. A. Downs. Chicago, IL: Markham.

Drake, Sinclair and Horace Cayton. 1945. *Black Metropolis.* 2 vols. New York: Harper and Row.

Du Bois, W. E. B. 1898. "The Study of the Negro Problem." *Annals, AAPSS* I (1): 1-23.

____. 1899. (Reprinted 1967). *The Philadelphia Negro.* New York: Shocken Books.

____. 1903. (Reprinted 1982). *The Souls of Black Folk.* New York: Signet, New American Library.

____. 1909. (Reprinted 1970). *The Negro American Family.* Cambridge, MA: The MIT Press.

Duncan, Greg. J. 1992. "The Disappearing Middle-Class." Testimony Before the U.S. House of Representatives Select Committee on Children, Youth and Families. 102nd Cong., 2d Sess., 12 February, Washington, DC , 186-206.

Edwards, Ozzie I. 1976. "Components of Academic Success: A Profile of Achieving Black Adolescents." *Journal of Negro Education*, 45 (4): 408-22.

Elliott, D. S. and D. Huizinga. 1983. "Social Class and Delinquent Behavior in a National Youth Panel: 1976-1980." *Criminology* 21 (2): 149-77.

Elliott, D. S., S. S. Ageton, D. Huizinga, B. A. Knowles, and R. J. Canter. 1983. *The Prevalence and Incidence of Delinquent Behavior: 1976-1980.* Boulder, CO: Behavioral Research Institute.

Ellsworth, Scott. 1982. *Death in A Promised Land: The Tulsa Race Riot of 1921.* Baton Rouge, LA: Louisiana State University.

Ellwood, David T. 1988a. *Poor Support: Poverty in the American Family.* New York: Basic Books.

____. 1988b. "Statement." Testimony Before the U S. House of Representatives, Select Committee on Children, Youth, and Families, 100th Cong., 2d Sess. Washington, DC: U.S. Government Printing Office, 4-20.

Emery, Robert E. and Rex Forehand. 1994. "Parental Divorce and Children's Well Being." Pp. 64-99 in *Stress, Risk, and Resilience in Children and* Adolescents, ed. Robert J. Haggerty et al. New York: Cambridge University Press.

Farley, Reynolds and Walter R. Allen. 1987. *The Color Line and The Quality of Life in America.* New York: Russell Sage Foundation.

Fischer, Roger A. 1969. "Racial Segregation in Antebellum New Orleans." *American Historical Review* 74 (3): 926-37.

Fordham, Signithia and John U. Ogbu. 1986. "Black Students' School Success: Coping with the "Burden of 'Acting White." *The Urban Review* 18 (3): 176-206.

Fordham, Signithia. 1988. "Racelessness as a Factor in Black Students' School Success." *Harvard Educational Review* 58 (1): 54-84.

Fortes, M. 1967. "Kinship and Marriage Among the Ashanti." Pp. 252-84 in *African Systems of Kinship and Marriage*, ed. A. R. Radcliffe-Brown and D. Forde. London: Oxford University Press.

Foster, Herbert J. 1983. "African Patterns in the Afro-American Family." *Journal of Black Studies* 14 (2): 201-32.

Frazier, E. Franklin. 1926. "Three Scourges of the Negro Family." *Opportunity* 4 (43): 210-13, 234.

____. 1931. "Family Disorganization Among Negroes." *Opportunity* 9 (7): 204-7.

____. 1932. (1968 Reprint). *The Free Negro Family.* New York: Arno Press.

____. 1939. "The Present Status of the Negro Family in the United States." *Journal of Negro Education* 8 (3): 376-82.

____. 1950. "Problems and Needs of Negro Children and Youth Resulting from Family Disorganization. " *Journal of Negro Education* 19 (3): 269-77.

____. 1939. (Revised 1966). *The Negro Family in the United States.* Chicago, IL: University of Chicago Press.

____. 1957. *The Negro in the United States.* New York: MacMillan Company.

Freedman, Samuel G. 1993. *Upon This Rock: The Miracles of a Black Church.* New York: Harper/Collins.

Freeman, Richard B. and Harry Holtzer, eds. 1986. *The Black Youth Employment Crisis*. Chicago, IL: University of Chicago Press.

Furstenberg, Jr., Frank F. 1981. "Implicating the Family: Teenage Parenthood and Kinship Involvement." Pp. 131-64 in *Teenage Pregnancy in a Family Context*, ed. Theodora Ooms. Philadelphia, PA: Temple University Press.

Furstenberg, Jr., Frank F. and Charles A. Thrall. 1975. Counting the Jobless: The Impact of Job Rationing on the Measurement of Unemployment," *Annals, AAPSS* 418 (March): 45-59.

Furstenberg, Jr., Frank F., Theodore Hershberg, and Modell, John. 1975. "The Origins of the Female-Headed Black Family." *Journal of Interdisciplinary History* 6 (2): 211-33.

Furstenberg, Jr., Frank F., Christine W. Nord, James L. Peterson, and Nicholas Zill. 1983. "The Life Course of Children of Divorce: Marital Disruption and Parental Contact." *American Sociological Review* 8 (5): 656-68.

Furtstenberg, Jr., Frank F., and Christine W. Nord. 1985. "Parenting Apart: Patterns of Childrearing After Marital Disruption." *Journal of Marriage and the Family* 47 (4): 893-904.

Furstenberg, Jr., Frank F., S. Phillip Morgan, and Paul D. Allison. 1987. "Paternal Participation and Children's Well-Being After Marital Disruption." *American Sociological Review* 52 (5): 695-701.

Gallup, Jr., George. 1995. "Religion in America." *The Public Interest* 6 (October/November): 1-8.

Gans, Herbert J. 1995. *The War Against the Poor: The Underclass and Antipoverty Policy*. New York: Basic Books.

Garbarino, James and Aaron Ebata. 1983. "The Significance of Ethnic and Cultural Differences in Child Maltreatment." *Journal of Marriage and the Family* 45 (4): 773-83.

Garmezy, Norman. 1994. "Reflections and Commentary on Risk, Resilience, and Development." Pp. 1-18 in *Stress, Risk and Resilience in Children and Adolescents*, ed. R. J. Haggerty, et al. New York: Cambridge University Press.

_____. 1987. "Stress, Competence and Development." *American Journal of Orthopsychiatry* 57 (2): 159-74.

Gary, Lawrence et al. 1983. *Stable Black Families*. Washington, DC: Howard University Institute for Urban Affairs and Research.

Geismar, Ludwig L. 1973. *555 Families: A Socio-Psychological Study of Young Families in Transition*. New Brunswick, NJ: Transaction Publishers.

Gibbs, Jewelle T., ed. 1988a. *Young, Black and Male in America: An Endangered Species*. Dover, MA: Auburn House.

_____. 1988b. "Health and Mental Health of Young Black Males." Pp. 219-57 in *Young Black and Male in America*, ed. J. T. Gibbs. Dover, MA: Auburn House.

_____. 1985a "Can We Continue to be Color-blind and Class-bound?" *The Counseling Psychologist* 13 (3): 426-35.

_____. 1985b. "City Girls: Psychosocial Adjustment of Urban Black Adolescent Females." *Sage* 2: 28-36.

Gilbert, Roland and Cheo Tyehimba-Taylor. 1993. *The Ghetto Solution.* Waco, TX: WRS Publishers.

Gilkes, Cheryl T. 1980. " 'Holding Back the Ocean with a Broom': Black Women and Community Work. Pp. 217-31 in *The Black Woman,* ed. La Frances Rodgers-Rose. Beverly Hills, CA: Sage Publications.

Gillespie, Bonnie J. 1976. "Black Grandparents: Childhood Socialization."*Journal of Afro-American Issues* 4 (3-4): 432-41.

Giovannoni, Jeanne M. and Andrew Billingsley. 1970. "Child Neglect Among the Poor: A Study of Parental Adequacy in Families of Three Ethnic Groups." *Child Welfare* 49 (4): 196-204.

Gite, Lloyd. 1994. "The New Agenda of the Black Church: Economic Development for Black America," *Community News* 7 (1): 1, 7, 9, 10. (Michigan State University School of Urban Affairs Newsletter)

Glasgow, Douglas G. 1981. *The Black Underclass.* New York: Vintage Books.

Glazer, Nathan. 1975. *Affirmative Discrimination.* New York: Basic Books.

Glazer, Nathan and Daniel Moynihan. 1963. *Beyond the Melting Pot.* Cambridge, MA: The MIT Press.

Goings, Kenneth and Raymond A. Mohl, eds. 1996. *The New African American Urban History.* Thousand Oaks, CA: Sage Publications.

Goodwin, Leonard. 1983. *Causes and Cures of Welfare:New Evidence on the Social Psychology of the Poor.* Lexington, MA: Lexington Books.

Groves, Paul A. 1974. "The 'Hidden' Population: Washington Alley Dwellers in the Late Nineteenth Century," *The Professional Geographer* 26 (3): 270-76.

Gurak, Douglas, David Smith, and Mary Goldsen. 1982. *The Minority Foster Child: A Comparative Study of Hispanic, Black, and White Children.* New York: Hispanic Research Center, Fordham University.

Gurin, Patricia and Edgar Epps. 1975. *Black Consciousness, Identity, and Achievement.* New York: John Wiley Sons.

Gurin, Patricia, Gerald Gurin, Rosina C. Lao and Muriel Beattie. 1969. "Internal-External Control in the Motivational Dynamics of Negro Youth." *Journal of Social Issues* 25 (3): 29-53.

Gutman, Herbert G. 1976. *The Black Family in Slavery and Freedom: 1750-1925.* New York: Vintage Books

Hagen, Duana Q. 1983. "The Relationship Between Job Loss and Physical and Mental Illness." *Hospital and Community Psychiatry* 34 (5): 438-41.

Haggerty, Robert J., Lonnie R. Sherrod, Norman Garmezy, and Michael Rutter, eds. 1994. *Stress, Risk, and Resilience in Children and Adolescents: Processes, Mechanisms and Interventions.* New York: Cambridge University Press.

Hagy, James W. 1978. "Black Business Women in Antebellum Charleston." *The Journal of Negro History* 62 (1-2): 42-44.

Hakim, Catherine. 1982. "The Social Consequences of High Unemployment," *Journal of Social Policy* 11 (4): 433-67.

Hale-Benson, Janice E. 1982. *Black Children: Their Roots, Culture, and Learning Styles*. Baltimore, MD: Johns Hopkins University Press.

Hall, Ethel H. and Gloria C. King. 1982. "Working with the Strengths of Black Families." *Child Welfare* 61 (8): 536-44.

Hamel, H., M. Goldberg, and T. Gavett. 1970. "Wage Expectations" in *Youth Unemployment and Minimum Wages*. BLS Bulletin No. 1657. Washington, DC: Bureau of Labor Statistics.

Handler, Joel F. 1995. *The Poverty of Welfare Reform*. New Haven, CT: Yale University Press.

Hanson, Shirley, Marsha Heims, Doris Julian, and Marvin Sussman, eds. 1995. "Single Parent Families: Diversity, Myths and Realities, Part One and Part Two." *Marriage and Family Review* 20 (1-2 and 3-4).

Harley, Sharon and Rosalyn Terborg-Penn. eds. 1978. *The Afro-American Woman: Struggles and Images*. Port Washington, NY: Kennikat Press.

Harris, Louis and Associates. 1989. *The Unfinished Agenda on Race in America*. New York: NAACP Legal Defense and Educational Fund.

Harris, M. A. 1968. *A Negro History Tour of Manhattan*. New York: Greenwood Publishing Corporation.

Harris, William. 1976. "Work and the Family in Black Atlanta, 1880." *Journal of Social History* 9 (3): 319-30.

Harrison, Algae O. et al. 1990. "Family Ecologies of Ethnic Minority Children." *Child Development* 61: 347-62.

Hartman, Chester. ed. 1997. *Double Exposure: Poverty and Race in America*. Armonk, New York: M. E. Sharpe.

Harvey, Aminifu R. 1985. "Traditional African Culture as the Basis for the Afro-American Church in America." Pp. 1-22 in *The Black Family: An Afrocentric Perspective*, ed. A. R. Harvey. New York: United Church of Christ Commission on Racial Justice.

Harvey, Aminifu R. and Antoinette A. Coleman. 1997. "An Afrocentric Program for African American Males in the Juvenile Justice System." Pp. 197-211 in *Child Welfare* 76 (1), eds. S. Jackson and S. Brissett-Chapman.

Hatchett, Shirley et al. 1991. "Family Life." pp. 46-83 in *Life in Black America*, ed. James Jackson. Newbury Park, CA: Sage Publications.

Hayes, William C. and Charles H. Mindel. 1973. "Extended Kinship Relations in Black and White Families." *Journal of Marriage and the Family* 35 (1): 51-57.

Heiss, Jerold. 1975. *The Case of the Black Family*. New York: Columbia University Press.

Hendrix-Wright, Beverly. 1981. "Influences on Self Esteem: Internal Versus External Control and Racial Group Identification," *Journal of Social and Behavioral Sciences* 27 (1): 12-22.

Hershberg, Theodore. 1971-72. "Free Blacks in Antebellum Philadelphia: A Study of Ex-Slaves, Freeborn and Socioeconomic Decline." *Journal of Social History* 5 (2): 183-207.

Hershey, Jr., Robert D. 1993. "Jobless Rate Underestimated, U.S. Says, Citing Survey Bias." *New York Times* (17 November): 1, D-2.

Herskovits, Melville J. 1938-39. "The Ancestry of the American Negro." *American Scholar* 8 (1): 84-94.

____. 1941. *The Myth of the Negro Past.* Boston, MA: Beacon Press.

Herzog, Elizabeth. 1970. "Social Stereotypes and Social Research." *Journal of Social Issues* 26 (3): 109-25.

Hill, Reuben and Donald A. Hansen. 1960. "The Identification of Conceptual Frameworks Utilized in Family Study." *Marriage and Family Living* 22 (4): 299-311.

Hill, Robert B. 1972. *The Strengths of Black Families.* New York: Emerson Hall.

____. 1977. *Informal Adoption Among Black Families.* Washington, DC: National Urban League Research Department.

____. 1980. *Merton's Role Types and Paradigm of Deviance.* New York: Arno Press and New York Times.

____. 1981. *Economic Policies and Black Progress.* Washington, DC: National Urban League Research Department.

____. 1983. "Comparative Socio-Economic Profiles of Caribbean and Non-Caribbean Blacks in the United States." Unpublished Paper.

____. 1988. "Structural Discrimination: The Unintended Consequences of Institutional Processes." Pp. 353-375 in *Surveying Social Life*, ed. Hubert J. O'Gorman. Middletown, CT: Wesleyan University Press.

____. 1989. "Critical Issues for Black Families by the Year 2000." Pp. 41-61 in *The State of Black America, 1989*, ed. Janet Dewart. New York: National Urban League.

____. 1990. "Economic Forces, Structural Discrimination, and Black Family Instability." Pp. 87-105 in *Black Families*, eds. Harold E. Cheatham and James B. Stewart. New Brunswick, NJ: Transaction Publishers.

____. 1992. "Urban Redevelopment: Developing Effective Targeting Strategies." Pp. 197-211 in *The State of Black America, 1992*, ed. Billy J. Tidwell. New York: National Urban League.

____. 1994. "The Role of the Black Church in Community and Economic Development Activities." Pp. 149-59 in *The Black Church*, ed. Andrew Billingsley. *National Journal of Sociology* 8 (Summer/Winter).

____. 1997. "Social Welfare Policies and African American Families." Pp. 349-363 in *Black Families*, ed. Harriette P. McAdoo. Thousand Oaks, CA: Sage Publications.

Hill, Robert B. with Andrew Billingsley, Eleanor Engram, Michelene Malson, Roger Rubin, Carol B. Stack, James B. Stewart, and James E. Teele. 1993. *Research on the African American Family: A Holistic Perspective.* Westport, CT: Auburn House.

Horton, James O. 1993. *Free People of Color.* Washington, DC: Smithsonian Press.

Horton, James O. and Lois E. Horton. 1979. *Black Bostonians: Family Life and Community Struggle in the Antebellum North.* New York: Holmes and Meier.

Hunt, Larry L. and Janet G. Hunt. 1975. "Race and the Father-Son Connection." *Social Problems* 23 (10): 35-52.

Hurstfield, Jennifer. 1978. "Internal Colonialism: White, Black, and Chicano Self-Conceptions." *Ethnic and Racial Studies* 1 (1): 60-79.

Hutchinson, Earl Ofari. 1992. *Black Fatherhood: The Guide to Male Parenting.* Los Angeles, CA: IMPACT! Publications.

_____. 1994. *The Assassination of the Black Male.* Los Angeles, CA: Middle Passage Press.

Hyman, Herbert and John Reed. 1969. "Black Matriarchy Reconsidered." *Public Opinion Quarterly* 33 (3): 346-54.

Institute for Urban Research. 1993. *Evaluation of Project 2000.* Baltimore, MD: Morgan State University.

_____. 1996. *Evaluation of MAAT CSAP-Rites of Passage Program.* Baltimore, MD: Morgan State University.

Jackson, Anthony, ed. 1982. *Black Families and the Medium Television.* Ann Arbor, MI: University of Michigan.

Jackson, James S., ed. 1991. *Life in Black America.* Newbury Park, CA: Sage Publications.

Jackson, Sondra and Sheryl Brissett-Chapman, eds. 1997. "Perspectives on Serving African American Children," *Child Welfare* 76 (1), Special Issue.

James, Portia P. 1989. *The Real McCoy: African-American Invention and Innovation, 1619-1930.* Washington, DC: Anacostia Museum. Smithsonian Institution Press.

Jarrett, Robin L. 1994. "Living Poor: Family Life Among Single Parent African American Women." *Social Problems* 41 (1): 30-49.

Jarrett, Robin L. 1995. "Growing Up Poor: The Family Experiences of Socially Mobile Youth in Low-Income African American Neighborhoods." *Journal of Adolescent Research* 10 (1): 111-35.

Jayakody, Rukmalie, Linda Chatters and Robert Taylor. 1993. "Family Support to Single and Married African American Mothers: Financial, Emotional and Child Care Assistance." *Journal of Marriage and the Family* 55 (2): 261-76.

Jeff, Jr., Morris F. X. 1994. "Afrocentrism and African American Males." Pp. 99-118 in *Nurturing Young Black Males,* ed. Ronald Mincy. Washington, DC: Urban Institute Press.

Jeffers, Camille. 1967. *Living Poor.* Ann Arbor, MI: Ann Arbor Publishing.

Jencks, Christopher and Paul E. Peterson, eds. 1991. *The Urban Underclass.* Washington, DC: The Brookings Institution.

Johnson, Charles S. 1930. *The Negro in American Civilization.* New York: Henry Holt and Company.

Johnson, James W. 1930. (1968 Reprint). *Black Manhattan.* New York: Arno Press.

Jones, Faustine C. 1981. "External Crosscurrents and Internal Diversity: An Assessment of Black Progress, 1960-1980."*Daedalus* (Spring): 71-102.

Jones, Reginald. 1980. *Black Psychology.* New York: Harper and Row.

Kandel, Denise B. 1971. "Race, Maternal Authority, and Adolescent Aspiration." *American Journal of Sociology* 76: 999-1020.

Kaplan, H. Roy and Curt Tausky. 1972. "Work and the Welfare Cadillac." *Social Problems* 19 (4): 469-83.

Karenga, Maulana. 1982. *Introduction to Black Studies.* Los Angeles, CA: Kawaida.

____. 1986. "Social Ethics and the Black Family." *The Black Scholar* 17: 41-54.

Katz, Michael B. ed. 1993. *The Underclass Debate: Views from History.* Princeton, NJ: Princeton University Press.

Kellam, Sheppard G. et al. 1982. "The Long-Term Evolution of the Family Structure of Teenage and Older Mothers." *Journal of Marriage and the Family* 44 (3): 539-54.

Kenyatta, M. 1983. "In Defense of the Black Family." *Monthly Review* 2: 12-21.

Kim, Marlene. 1996. "The Working Poor and Welfare Recipiency." *Poverty & Race* 5 (Jan/Feb): 7-8.

King, James R. 1976. "African Survivals in the Black American Family." *Journal of Afro-American Issues* 4 (2): 153-67.

Korbin, J. E., ed. 1981. *Child Abuse and Neglect: Cross-Cultural Perspectives.* Berkeley, CA: University of California Press.

Kunjufu, Jawanza. 1985. *Countering the Conspiracy to Destroy Black Boys. Vol.1.* Chicago, IL: African-American Images.

____. 1986. *Motivating and Preparing Black Youth to Work.* Chicago, IL: African-American Images.

____. 1994. *Adam! Where Are You? Why Most Black Men Do Not Go to Church.* Chicago, IL: African-American Images.

Kramer, Michael. 1995. "The Myth About Welfare Moms." *Time* (3 July): 21.

Ladner, Joyce. 1971. *Tomorrow's Tomorrow: The Black Woman.* Garden City, NY: Doubleday & Company.

Landry, Bart. 1978. "Growth of the Black Middle Class in the 1960's." *Urban League Review* 3 (2): 68-82.

____. 1987. *The New Black Middle Class.* Berkeley, CA.: University of California Press.

Larson, Tom. 1988. "Employment and Unemployment of Young Black Males." Pp. 97-128 in *Young, Black, and Male in America,* ed. J. T. Gibbs. Dover, MA: Auburn House.

Lawson, Bill E., ed. 1992. *The Underclass Question*. Philadelphia, PA: Temple University Press.

Lee, Courtland C. 1994. "Adolescent Development." Pp. 33-44 in *Nurturing Young Black Males*, ed. Ronald Mincy. Washington, DC: Urban Institute Press.

Leigh, Wilhelmina A., ed. 1991. "Special Issue on Housing." *Review of Black Political Economy* 19 (3-4).

Lemann, Nicholas. 1991. *The Promised Land*. New York: Random House.

Le Prohn, N. 1994. "The Role of the Kinshp Foster Parent." *Children and Youth Services Review*, 16 (2).

Levine, James A. and Edward W. Pitt. 1995. *New Expectations: Community Strategies for Responsible Fatherhood*. New York: Families and Work Institute.

Levitan, Sar, William B. Johnston, and Robert Taggart. 1975. *Still A Dream: The Changing Status of Blacks Since 1960*. Cambridge, MA: Harvard University Press.

Lewis, Diane K. 1975. "The Black Family: Socialization and Sex Roles." *Phylon* 36 (2): 221-37.

Lewis, Hylan. 1967. "Culture, Class, and Family Life Among Low-Income Urban Negroes." Pp. 149-72 in *Employment, Race and Poverty*, ed. Arthur Ross and Herbert Hill. New York: Harcourt, Brace & World.

Lewis, Jerry M. and John G. Looney. 1983. The Long Struggle: *Well Functioning Working-Class Black Families*. New York: Brunner/Mazel.

Lewis, Oscar. 1959. *Five Families*. New York: Basic Books.

____. 1966. *La Vida*. New York: Random House.

Lincoln, C. Eric and Lawrence Mamiya. 1990. *The Black Church in the African American Experience*. Durham, NC: Duke University Press.

Logan, Sadye L., ed. 1996. *The Black Family: Strengths, Self-Help and Positive Change*. Boulder, CO: Westview Press.

Loury, Glen. 1984. "Internally-Directed Action for Black Community Development," *Review of Black Political Economy* 13 (1-2): 31-46.

Luthar, Suniya S. and Edward Zigler. 1991. "Vulnerability and Competence: A Review of Research on Resilience in Childhood." *American Journal of Orthopsychiatry* 6 (1): 6-22.

Malson, Michelene R. 1983. "Black Women's Sex Roles: The Social Context for a New Ideology." *Journal of Social Issues* 39 (3): 101-13.

____. 1986. *Understanding Black Single-Parent Families: Stresses and Strengths*. Wellesley, MA: Wellesley Collge Center for Developmental Services and Studies.

Mann, Wilhelmina. 1988. "Supportive Roles of Significant Others in Black Families." Pp. 270-283 in *Black Families*, ed. Harriette P. McAdoo. Beverly Hills, CA: Sage Publications.

Martin, Elmer P. and Joanne M. Martin. 1978. *The Black Extended Family*. Chicago, IL: University of Chicago Press.

_____. 1995. *Social Work and the Black Experience*. Washington, DC: National Association of Social Workers.

Martineau, William H. 1977. "Informal Social Ties Among Urban Black Americans." *Journal of Black Studies* 8 (1): 83-104.

Marx, Karl and Frederich Engels. 1932. *Manifesto of the Communist Party*. New York: International Publishers.

Mason, J. and C. Williams. 1985. "The Adoption of Minority Children." Pp. 81-93 in *Adoption of Children with Special Needs*. Washington, DC: American Bar Association.

Massey, Douglass S. and Nancy A. Denton. 1993. *American Apartheid: Segregation and the Making of the Underclass.the Underclass*. Cambridge, MA: Harvard University Press.

Maynard, Joan and Gwen Cottman. 1983. *Weeksville: Then and Now*. Brooklyn, New York: Society for the Preservation of Weeksville & Bedford-Stuyvesant History.

Mbiti, J. 1970. *African Religions and Philosophy*. Garden City, NJ: Anchor.

McAdoo, Harriette P. 1983. "Extended Family Support of Single Black Mothers: Final Report." Washington, DC: National Institute of Mental Health.

_____. 1985. "Racial Attitude and Self-Concept of Young Black Children Over Time." Pp. 213-42 in *Black Children*, ed. H. McAdoo and J. McAdoo. Beverly Hills, CA: Sage Publications.

_____. ed. 1988. *Black Families*. Beverly Hills, CA: Sage Publications.

_____. ed. 1991. *Family Ethnicity. Strength in Diversity*. Newbury Park, CA: Sage Publications.

McDaniel, Antonio. 1990. "The Power of Culture: A Review of the Idea of Africa's Influence on Family Structure in Antebellum America." *Journal of Family History* 15 (2): 225-38.

_____. 1994. "Historical Racial Differences in Living Arrangements of Children." *Journal of Family History* 19 (1): 57-77.

McIntyre, Charshee C. 1992. *Criminalizing a Race: Free Blacks During Slavery*. Queens, New York: Kayode Publications.

McKenry, P. C. 1990a. "Drug Abuse." Pp. 45-56 in *Black Adolescence,* ed. Consortium for Research on Black Adolescence. Boston, MA: G. K. Hall.

_____. 1990b. "Suicide." Pp. 57-68 in *Black Adolescence,* ed. Consortium for Research on Black Adolescence, Boston, MA: G. K. Hall.

McKenry, P, J. Everett, H. Ramseur, and C. Carter. 1989. "Research on Black Adolescents: A Legacy of Cultural Bias." *Journal of Adolescent Research* 4 (2): 254-64.

McLanahan, Sara S. 1995. "The Consequences of Nonmarital Childrearing for Women, Children and Society." Pp. 229-39 in *Report to Congress on Out-of-Wedlock Childbearing*. Washington, DC: National Center for Health Statistics.

McPhatter, Anna R. 1997. "Cultural Competence in Child Welfare." *Child Welfare* 76 (1): 255-78.

McRoy, Ruth G., Zena Oglesby and Helen Grape. 1997. "Achieving Same-Race Adoptive Placements for African American Children: Culturally Sensitive Practice Approaches." *Child Welfare* 76 (1): 85-104.

Merton, Robert K. 1948. "Discrimination and the American Creed." Pp. 99-126 in *Discrimination and the National Welfare*, ed. R. M. McIver. New York: Harper.

_____. 1957. *Social Theory and Social Structure*. Glencoe, Ill.: Free Press.

_____. 1964. "Anomie, Anomia and Social Interaction: Contexts of Deviant Behavior." Pp. 213-42 in *Anomie and Deviant Behavior*, ed. M. B. Clinard. New York: Free Press.

Merva, Mary and Richard Fowles. 1992. "Effects of Diminished Opportunities on Social Stress: Heart Attacks, Strokes and Crime." Washington, DC: The Economic Policy Institute.

Miller, Andrew T. 1993. "Social Science, Social Policy, and the Heritage of African-American Families." Pp. 254-89 in *The 'Underclass' Debate: Views from History*, ed. Michael B. Katz. Princeton, NJ: Princeton University Press.

Millette, Robert E. 1990. "West Indian Families in the United States," Pp. 301-17 in *Black Families*, ed. Harold E. Cheatham and James B. Stewart. New Brunswick, NJ: Transaction Publishers.

Mincy, Ronald B. ed. 1994. *Nurturing Young Black Males*. Washington, DC: Urban Institute Press.

Minkler, Meredith, Kathleen Roe and Marilyn Price. 1992. "The Physical and Emotional Health of Grandmothers Raising Grandchildren in the Crack Cocaine Epidemic." *The Gerontologist* 32 (6): 752-61.

Model, Suzanne. 1995. "West Indian Prosperity: Fact or Fiction?" *Social Problems* 42 (4): 535-52.

Moffitt, Robert A. 1995. "The Effect of the Welfare System on Nonmarital Childbearing." Pp. 167-176 in *Report to Congress on Out-of-Wedlock Childbearing*. Washington, DC: National Center for Health Statistics.

Moore, Kristin A. and Dana Glei. 1995. "Taking the Plunge: An Examination of Positive Youth Development." *Journal of Adolescent Research* 10 (1): 15-40.

Morgan, S. Phillip et al. 1993. "Racial Differences in Household and Family Structure at the Turn of the Century." *American Journal of Sociology* 98 (4): 798-828.

Moynihan, Daniel P. 1967. "The Negro Family: A Case for National Action." Pp. 41-124 in *The Moynihan Report and the Politics of Controversy*, ed. Lee Rainwater and William L. Yancey. Cambridge, MA: The MIT Press.

Murray, Charles. 1984. *Losing Ground: American Social Policy, 1950-1980*. New York: Basic Books.

Myrdal, Gunner. 1944. *An American Dilemma: Vol. 2*. New York: Harper Brothers.

_____. 1963. *Challenge to Affluence*. New York: Pantheon.

National Center for Education Statistics. 1991. *Private Schools in the United States: A Statistical Profile with Comparisons to Public Schools.* Washington, DC: U.S. Government Printing Office.

____. 1992. *Historically Black Colleges and Universities: 1976-1990.* Washington, DC: U.S. Government Printing Office.

____. 1995. "1993 National Household Education Survey Public Use Data," Washington, D.C.: U.S. Department of Education.

National Center for Health Statistics. 1995. *Report to Congress on Out-of-Wedlock Childbearing.* Washington, DC: U.S. Department of Health and Human Services.

____. 1990. "Adoption in the 1980." *Advance Data* 181 (5 January) Washington, DC: U.S. Government Printing Office.

____. 1995a. "Health-Risk Behaviors Among Our Nation's Youth: United States, 1992." *Vital and Health Statistics* 10 (192). Washington, DC: U.S. Government Printing Office.

____. 1995b. "Births to Unmarried Mothers: United States, 1980-92." *Vital and Health Statistics* 21 (53). Washington, DC: U.S. Government Printing Office.

____. 1995c. *Report to Congress on Out-of-Wedlock Childbearing.* Washington, DC: U.S. Government Printing Office.

National Institute on Drug Abuse. 1991a. *National Household Survey on Drug Abuse: Population Estimates, 1990.* Washington, DC: U.S. Government Printing Office.

____. 1991b. *National Household Survey on Drug Abuse: Main Findings, 1990.* Washington, DC: U.S. Government Printing Office.

____. 1995. *National Household Survey on Drug Abuse: Main Findings, 1994.* Washington, D.C.: U.S. Government Printing Office.

National Urban League. 1992. *Perils of Neglect: Black Unemployment in the '90's.* Washington, DC: National Urban League Research Department.

Nettles, Saundra M. and Joseph H. Pleck. 1994. "Risk, Resilience, and Development: The Multiple Ecologies of Black Adolescents in the United States." Pp. 147-81 in *Stress, Risk and Resilience in Children and Adolescents: Processes, Mechanisms, and Interventions*, ed. R. J. Haggerty, L. R. Sherrod, N. Garmezy, and M. Rutter. Cambridge, MA: Cambridge University Press.

Newman, Dorothy K. et al. 1978. *Protest, Politics and Prosperity.* New York: Pantheon Books.

Nobles, Wade. 1974. "African Root and American Fruit: The Black Family." *Journal of Social and Behavioral Sciences* 20 (2): 52-63.

Offner, Paul. 1995. "Welfare Didn't Do It." *Washington Post* (12 March), C-7.

Oliver, Melvin and Thomas Shapiro. 1995. *Black Wealth/White Wealth.* New York: Routledge.

Osofsky, Gilbert. 1968 "The Enduring Ghetto." *Journal of American History* 55 (2): 243-55.

Palmer, John L. and Isabel V. Sawhill, eds. 1984. *The Reagan Record.* Cambridge, MA: Ballinger.

Palmer, Ransford W. 1974. "A Decade of West Indian Migration to the United States, 1962-1972: An Economic Analysis." *Social and Economic Studies* 23(4): 571-87.

Parsons, Talcott and Robert Bales. 1955. *Family, Socialization and Interaction Process.* New York: Free Press.

Payton, Isabelle S. 1982. "Single-Parent Households: An Alternative Approach." *Family Economics Review* (Winter): 11-16.

Pearce, Diana and Harriette P. McAdoo. 1981. *Women and Children: Alone and in Poverty.* Washington, DC: National Advisory Council on Economic Opportunity.

Perkins, Useni Eugene. 1993. *Mothers Are Not Broken Homes.* Chicago, IL: Association for the Positive Development of Youth.

Pincus, Fred. L. 1996. "Discrimination Comes in Many Forms: Individual, Institutional and Structural." Pp. 186-94 in "Multiculturalism and Diversity in Higher Education." ed. Jack Meacham. *American Behavioral Scientist* 40 (2).

Pinderhughes, Elaine B. 1982. "Family Functioning of Afro-Americans." *Social Work,* 27 (1): 91-96

Pinkney, Alphonso. 1984. *The Myth of Black Progress.* Cambridge, MA: Cambridge University Press.

Piore, Michael. 1979. *Birds of Passage.* Cambridge, MA: Cambridge University Press.

Pleck, Elizabeth H. 1979. *Boston, 1865-1900: Black Migration and Poverty.* New York; Academic Press.

Ploski, Harry A. and James Williams, eds. 1983. *The Negro Almanac.* New York: Bellwether Publishers.

Poulin, John E. 1991. "Racial Differences in the Use of Drugs and Alcohol Among Low-Income Youth and Young Adults." *Journal of Sociology and Social Welfare* 18 (3): 159-66.

Powell, Frances J. 1980. "A Study of the Structure of the Freed Black Family in Washington, D.C., 1850-1880." Ph.D. diss., Catholic University of America.

Powell, G. 1973. *Black Monday's Children: The Psychological Effects of School Desegregation on Southern School Children.* New York: Appleton-Century-Croft.

Prohansky, Harold and Peggy Newton. 1968. "The Nature and Meaning of Negro Self-Identity." Pp. 178-218 in *Social Class, Race and Psychological Development,* ed. Martin Deutsch et al. New York: Holt, Rinehart and Winston.

Ramseur, H. P. 1989. "Psychological Health." Pp. 17-26 in *Black Adolescence,* ed. Consortium for Research in Black Adolescence. Boston, MA: G. K. Hall.

_____. 1990. "Psychologically Healthy Black Adults: A Review of Research and Theory." Pp. 215-41 in *Black Adult Development and Aging,* ed. Reginald Jones. Berkeley, CA: Cobbs and Henry.

Rank, Mark R. 1994a. "A View from the Inside Out: Recipients' Perceptions of Welfare." *Journal of Sociology and Social Welfare* 21 (2): 27-47.

_____. 1994b. *Living on the Edge: The Realities of Welfare in America*. New York: Columbia University Press.

Raspberry, William. 1997. "Society's Last Line of Defense." *Washington Post* (6 January), A-17.

Rebach, Howard M., Catherine Bolek, Katherine Williams and Robert Russell. 1992. *Substance Abuse Among Ethnic Minorities in America: A Critical Annotated Bibliography*. New York: Garland.

Reed, Gregory. 1994. "Faith Initiatives of Church Community Development Corporations." *Community News* 7 (1): 3, 5, 8. (Michigan State University)

Reich, Robert B. 1994. "The Fracturing of the Middle Class." *New York Times* (31 August), A-19.

Reid, Ira D. A. 1939. *The Negro Immigrant: His Background, Characteristics and Social Adjustment, 1899-1937*. New York: Columbia University Press.

Reissman, Frank. 1964. "Low-Income Culture: The Strengths of the Poor." *Journal of Marriage and the Family* 26 (4): 417-21.

Resource Center on Child Abuse and Neglect, Region VI. 1981. "Beneath the Tip of the Iceberg: A Summary of Findings from the National Study of the Incidence and Severity of Child Abuse and Neglect." *Perspectives*. (University of Texas at Austin)

Ricketts, Erol. 1989. "The Origin of Black Female-Headed Families." *Focus* 12 (1): 32-36.

Rodgers-Rose, La Frances, ed. 1980. *The Black Woman*. Beverly Hills, CA: Sage Publications.

Rosenberg, Morris and Roberta Simmons. 1972. *Black and White Self-Esteem: The Urban School Child*. Washington, DC: American Sociological Association.

Rosenthal, Robert and Lenore Jacobson. 1968. "Self-Fulfilling Prophecies in the Classroom: Teachers' Expectations as Unintended Determinants of Pupils' Intellectual Competence." Pp. 219-53 in *Social Class, Race and Psychological Development*, ed. Martin Deutsch, Irwin Katz, and Arthur Jensen. New York: Holt, Rinehart and Winston.

Rotter. J. B. 1966. "Generalized Expectancies for Internal Versus External Control of Reinforcement." *Psychological Monographs* 80: 1-28.

Royce, David D. and Gladys T. Turner. 1980. "Strengths of Black Families: A Black Community's Perspective." *Social Work* 25: 407-9.

Ruggles, Steven. 1994. "The Origins of African-American Structure." *American Sociological Review* 59 (1): 136-51.

Rutter, Michael. 1994. "Stress Research: Accomplishments and Tasks Ahead." Pp. 354-85 in *Stress, Risk and Resilience in Children and Adolescents*, ed. R. Haggerty et al. Cambridge, MA: Cambridge University Press.

_____. 1987. "Psychosocial Resilience and Protective Mechanisms." *American Journal of Orthopsychiatry* 57 (3): 316-31.

Sandven, Karl and Michael D. Resnick. 1990. "Informal Adoption Among Black Adolescent Mothers." *American Journal of Orthopsychiatry* 60 (2): 210-24.

Scheiner, Seth M. 1965. *Negro Mecca: A History of the Negro in New York City, 1865-1920.* New York: New York University Press.

Scheirer, Mary Ann. 1983. "Household Structure Among Welfare Families: Correlates and Consequences." *Journal of Marriage and the Family* 45 (4): 761-71.

Schorr, Lisbeth B. 1988. *Within Our Reach: Breaking the Cycle of Disadvantage.* New York: Doubleday and , Anchor Press.

Sedlak, Andrea J. and Diane D. Broadhurst. 1996. "Executive Summary of the Third National Incidence Study of Child Abuse and Neglect." U.S. Department of Health and Human Services.

Seltzer, Judith A. and Suzanne M. Bianchi. 1988. "Children's Contact with Absent Parents." *Journal of Marriage and the Family* 50 (3): 663-77.

Sernett, Milton C., ed. 1985. *Afro-American Religious History: A Documentary Witness.* Durham, NC: Duke University Press.

Shipp, Sigmund C. 1997. "Winning Some Battles But Losing the War? Blacks and Urban Renewal in Greensboro, N. C., 1953-1965. Pp. 187-200 in *Urban Planning and the African American Community*, ed. June Thomas and Marsha Ritzdorf. Thousands Oaks, CA: Sage Publications.

Simmons, Roberta G. 1978. "Blacks and High Self-Esteem: A Puzzle." *Social Psychology* 41 (1): 54-57.

Slaughter, Diana T. and Gerald McWorter. 1985. "Social Origins and Early Features of the Scientific Study of Black Americans and Children." Pp. 5-18 in *Beginnings: The Social and Affective Development of Black Children,* ed. Margaret B. Spencer et al. Hillsdale, NJ: Lawrence Erlbaum Associates.

Slaughter, Diana T. and Edgar Epps. 1987. "The Home Environment and Academic Achievement of Black American Children and Youth: An Overview." *The Journal of Negro Education* 56 (1): 3-20.

Slaughter-Defoe, Diana T., Kathryn Nakagawa, Ruby Takanishi, and Deborah J. Johnson. 1990. "Toward Cultural/Ecological Perspectives on Schooling and Achievement in African and Asian-American Children." *Child Development* 61 (1): 363-83.

Sowell, Thomas. 1978. *Essays and Data on American Ethnic Groups.* Washington, DC: The Urban Institute.

Spencer, Margaret B. 1987. "Black Children's Ethnic Identity Formation: Risk and Resilience of Castelike Minorities." Pp. 103-16 in *Children's Ethnic Socialization*, ed. J. Phinney and M. J. Rotheram. Newbury Park, CA: Sage Publications.

_____. 1990. "Development of Minority Children." *Child Development* 61 (2): 267-269.

Spencer, Margaret, Geraldine Brookins and Walter Allen, eds. 1985. *Beginnings: The Social and Affective Development of Black Children.* Hillsdale, NJ: Erlbaum.

Stack, Carol. 1974. *All Our Kin: Strategies for Survival in a Black Community.* New York: Harper & Row.

_____. 1996. *Call to Home.* New York: Basic Books.

Staples, Robert and Leanor B. Johnson. 1993. *Black Families at the Crossroads: Challenges and Prospects.* San Francisco, CA: Jossey-Bass.

Steinberg, Stephen. 1989. *The Ethnic Myth.* Boston, MA: Beacon Press.

_____. 1995. *Turning Back: The Retreat from Racial Justice in American Thought and Policy.* Boston, MA: Beacon Press.

Stevens, Jr., Joseph H. 1984. "Black Grandmothers' and Black Adolescent Mothers' Knowledge About Parenting." *Developmental Psychology* 20 (6): 1017-25.

Stevenson, Harold W., Chuansheng Chen, and David H. Uttal. 1990. "Beliefs and Achievement: A Study of Black, White and Hispanic Children." *Child Development* 61 (2): 508-23.

Stevenson, Howard C. and Gary Renard. 1993. "Trusting Ole' Wise Owls: Therapeutic Use of Cultural Strengths in African American Families." *Professional Psychology: Research and Practice* 24 (4): 433-42.

Stewart, James B. and T. J. Hyclak. 1986. "The Effects of Immigrant, Women and Teenagers on the Relative Earnings of Black Males." *The Review of Black Political Economy* 15 (1): 93-101.

Stouffer, Samuel A., Paul F. Lazersfeld, and Abram Jaffe. 1937. *Research Memorandum on the Family in the Depression.* New York: Social Science Research Council.

Sudarkasa, Niara. 1975. "An Exposition on the Value Premises Underlying Black Family Studies." *Journal of National Medical Association* 67 (3): 235-39.

_____. 1980. "African and Afro-American Family Structure: A Comparison." *Black Scholar* 11 (8): 37-60.

_____. 1988. "Interpreting the African Heritage in Afro-American Family Organization." Pp. 27-43 in *Black Families,* ed. Harriette P. McAdoo. Newbury Park, CA: Sage Publications.

Sullivan, Leon H. 1969. *Build Brother Build.* Philadelphia, PA: Macrae Smith Company.

Sullivan, Mercer. 1985. *Teen Fathers in the Inner City.* New York: Ford Foundation.

Swan, Alex L. 1981. *Survival and Progress: The Afro-American Experience.* Westport, CT: Greenwood Press.

Taylor, Clarence. 1994. *The Black Churches of Brooklyn.* New York: Columbia University Press.

Taylor, Robert J. 1985. "The Extended Family as a Source of Support to Elderly Blacks." *The Gerontologist* 25 (5): 488-95.

Taylor, Robert J. and Linda Chatters. 1991. "Religious Life." Pp. 105-23 in *Life in Black America,* ed. James J. Jackson. Newbury Park, CA: Sage Publications.

Taylor, Ronald L. 1976. "Psychosocial Development Among Black Children and Youth." *American Journal of Orthopsychiatry* 46 (1): 4-19.

____. 1981. "Psychological Modes of Adaptation." Pp. 141-58 in *Black Men*, ed. Lawrency Gary. Beverly Hills, CA: Sage Publications.

____. 1995. *African-American Youth: Their Social and Economic Status in the United States*. Westport, CT: Praeger.

TenHouton, Warren D. 1970. "The Black Family: Myth and Reality." *Psychiatry* 33 (2): 145-73.

Testa, Mark and Marilyn Krogh. 1995. "The Effects of Employment on Marriage Among Black Males in Inner-City Chicago." Pp. 59-95 in *The Decline in Marriage Among African Americans*, ed. M. Belinda Tucker and Claudia Mitchell-Kernan. Thousand Oaks, CA: Russell Sage Foundation.

Thomas, Alexander and Sillen, Samuel. 1979. *Racism and Psychiatry*. Secaucus, NJ: The Citadel Press.

Thomas, Bettye C. 1974. "A Nineteenth Century Black Operated Shipyard, 1866-1884: Reflections Upon its Inception and Ownership." *Journal of Negro History* 59 (1): 1-12.

Thornton, Michael, Linda Chatters, Robert Taylor and Walter Allen. 1990. "Sociodemographic and Environmental Correlates of Racial Socialization by Black Parents." *Child Development* 61 (2): 401-409.

Tienda, Marta and Haya Stier. 1991. "Joblessness and Shiftlessness: Labor Force Activity." Pp. 135-54 in *The Urban Underclass*, ed. Christopher Jencks and Paul E. Peterson. Washington, DC: The Brookings Institution.

Tierney, Joseph P., J. B. Grossman and N. L. Resch. 1995. *Making A Difference: An Impact Study of Big Brothers/Big Sisters*. Philadelphia, PA: Public/Private Ventures.

Tolson, Timothy F. J. and Melvin Wilson. 1990. "The Impact of Two- and Three-Generational Black Family Structure on Perceived Family Climate." *Child Development* 61: 416-28.

Trotter, Jr., Joe William. 1996. "African Americans in the City: The Industrial Era, 1900-1950." Pp. 299-319 in *The New African American Urban History*, ed. Kenneth Goings and Raymond A. Mohl. Thousand Oaks, CA: Sage Publications.

____. 1993. "Blacks in the Urban North: The 'Underclass Question' in Historical Perspective." Pp. 55-81 in *The Underclass Debate*, ed. Michael Katz. Princeton, NJ: Princeton University Press.

Tucker, M. Belinda. 1985. "U.S. Ethnic Minorities and Drug Abuse: An Assessment of the Science and Practice."*International Journal of the Addictions* 20 (6-7): 1021-47.

Tucker, M. Belinda and Claudia Mitchell-Kernan. eds. 1995. *The Decline in Marriage Among African Americans*. New York: Russell Sage Foundation.

U. S. Bureau of the Census. 1992. "Household and Family Characteristics: March 1989 and March 1990." *Current Population Reports*. Series P-20, No. 447. Washington, DC: U.S. Government Printing Office.

U S. Children's Bureau. 1984. "Child Welfare Notes #3." U. S. Department of Health and Human Services.

U.S. Department of Health and Human Services. 1996. *Trends in the Well-Being of America's Children and Youth: 1996.* Washington, DC: Office of the Assistant Secretary for Planning and Evaluation.

Valentine, Charles. 1968. *Culture and Poverty: Critique and Counter-Proposals.* Chicago, IL: University of Chicago Press.

Warden, Ivan L. 1966. "Keys That Work." *Message* (January/February), 4-5.

Warfield-Coppock, Nsenga. 1992. "The Rites of Passage Movement: A Resurgence of African-Centered Practices for Socializing African American Youth." *Journal of Negro Education* 61 (4): 471-82.

Warner, W. Lloyd and Paul S. Lunt. 1942. *The Status of a Modern Community.* New Haven, CT: Yale University Press.

Wasserman, Herbert. 1972. "A Comparative Study of School Performance Among Boys From Broken and Intact Black Families," *Journal of Negro Education* 41 (2): 137-41.

Webb, Gary. 1996. "Dark Alliance," *San Jose Mercury News* (18-20 August) (Reprint of three-day series)

Werner, E. E. and R. S. Smith. 1982. *Vulnerable But Invincible: A Study of Resilient Children.* New York: McGraw-Hill.

Westat, Inc. 1992. "A National Evaluation of Title IV-E Foster Care Independent Living Programs for Youth." Phase 2 Final Report. Volume One. Washington, DC: U. S. Department of Health and Human Services.

White, Joseph L. and Thomas A. Parham. 1994. *The Psychology of Blacks.* Englewood Cliffs, NJ: Prentice Hall.

Williams, J. Allen and Robert Stockton. 1973. "Black Family Structures and Functions: An Empirical Examination of Some Suggestions Made by Billingsley." *Journal of Marriage and the Family* 35 (1): 39-49.

Williams, Kenton. 1987. "Cultural Diversity in Family Support: Black Families." Pp. 295-307 in *America's Family Support Programs,* ed. Sharon L. Kagan, Douglas R. Powell, B. Weissbourd, and Edward F. Zigler. New Haven, CT: Yale University Press.

Williams, Terry M. and William Kornblum. 1991. "A Portrait of Youth: Coming of Age in Harlem Public Housing." Pp. 187-207 in *The State of Black America, 1994,* ed. Janet Dewart. New York: National Urban League.

_____. 1994. *The Uptown Kids:Struggle and Hope in the Projects.* New York: G. P. Putnam & Sons.

Willie, Charles V. 1976. *A New Look at Black Families.* New York: General Hall.

Wilson, Dana and Sandra S. Chipungu, eds. 1996. "Kinship Care." *Child Welfare* 75 (5) (Special Issue).

Wilson, Jay. J. and Ron Wallace. 1992. *Black Wall Street: A Lost Dream.* Oklahoma: Black Wall St. Publishing Company.

Wilson, Karen R. and Walter R. Allen. 1987. "Explaining the Educational Attainment of Young Black Adults: Critical Familial and Extra-Familial Influences." *Journal of Negro Education* 56 (1): 64-76.

Wilson, Melvin N. 1984. "Mothers' and Grandmothers' Perception of Parental Behavior in Three-Generational Black Families." *Child Development* 55: 1333-39.

_____. 1986. "The Black Extended Family: An Analytical Consideration." *Developmental Psychology* 22 (2): 246-58.

Wilson, William J. 1978. *The Declining Significance of Race.* Chicago, IL: University of Chicago Press.

_____. 1987. *The Truly Disadvantaged: The Inner City, the Underclass and Public Policy.* Chicago, IL: University of Chicago Press.

_____. 1996. *When Work Disappears: The World of the New Urban Poor.* New York: Alfred A. Knopf.

Wimberly, Edward P. 1979. *Pastoral Care in the Black Church.* Nashville, TN: Abingdon Press.

Winfield, Linda F., ed. 1991a. "Resilience, Schooling and Development in African-American Youth." *Education and Urban Society* 24 (1) (Special Issue).

_____. 1991b. "Resilience, Schooling and Development in African-American Youth: A Conceptual Framework." *Education and Urban Society* 24 (1): 5-14.

Woodson, Carter G. 1925. *Free Negro Heads of Families in the United States in 1830.* Washington, DC: Association for the Study of Negro Life and History.

_____. 1972. "The Independent Church Movement." Pp. 61-85 in *The History of the Negro Church,* 3rd ed. Washington, DC: Association for the Study of Negro Life and History.

Woodson, Robert L. 1981. *A Summons to Life: Mediating Structures and the Prevention of Youth Crime.* Cambridge, MA: Ballinger.

_____. 1987. *On the Road to Economic Freedom: An Agenda for Black Progress.* Washington, DC: Regnery Gateway.

Young, Virginia H. 1970. "Family and Childhood in a Southern Negro Community." *American Anthropologist* 72 (2): 269-88.